"When my father died fourteen years ago, I quit my corporate job with the airlines and focused my life on a deep and dramatic search for Truth. That search led me to live with the Hopi Indians, and to travel to the mountains of Peru, the Philippines, Sri Lanka, Thailand, India, El Salvador and more. I learned that the most important thing I could do with the rest of my lifetime was to turn my attention back to humanity and bring love into action. Just by doing whatever I could to make that love practically visible to others, I would be contributing to the evolutionary force of the universe and help unleash a tidal wave of goodwill that will eventually sweep mankind collectively into a whole new state of Being. Bravo for Bettie, for that is precisely what she is doing on this planet. Mankind stands at the pivotal threshold of an evolutionary leap in consciousness. Bettie Youngs is helping thousands who are ready but unaware of how to start the positive spiral of change in their lives. By sharing examples of living love and compassion, which is exactly what *Taste-Berry Tales* is about, she is holding a new vision before the public, a vision which holds the key for a New Humanity."

Nancy L. Rivard, founder and president,
Airline Ambassadors International

"If, as Forrest Gump's momma suggested, 'life is like a box of chocolates,' Bettie Youngs knows what's inside all those delectable goodies: taste berries! Her hopeful brand of faith and optimism will entertain, inspire and delight even the most jaded of souls. Read *Taste-Berry Tales*—it will do your heart good. Give a copy to a loved one—and to your favorite sourpuss!"

Cathy Keating, first lady of Oklahoma

"Your words soothe suffering and create happiness."

Mother Teresa

"While we're led to believe that attaining material things creates fulfillment and happiness, *Taste-Berry Tales* points our attention to a more genuine and satisfying path: giving of ourselves and helping others. Bettie Youngs proclaims what I have discovered myself—giving is not a sacrifice but rather generates feelings of genuine contentment and satisfaction. Rejoice in reading this exciting book and 'taste' the true riches it offers."

Millard Fuller, founder and president, Habitat for Humanity International

"*Taste-Berry Tales* is simply a beautiful book. Bettie has distilled what's important and what's precious about life: It's impossible to sedate the longings of the soul. But the world is the sum of all our hearts, however we speak or understand that mystery, and so often the way of regaining our inner divine connection when we feel separated is to uplift someone else. The message within these stories demonstrates just how powerful that truth is."

James Redfield, *New York Times* bestselling author, *The Celestine Vision*

"Bettie Youngs has a unique ability to share optimism, generosity of spirit and hope with her readers. Whenever I read her books, I'm inspired to be kinder, more tolerant, more patient and more generous to others. Sometimes we need to remind ourselves of the importance of a smile, kind words and a helping hand—and know that they are contagious: the more you give, the more you get back. Imagine the effects in our homes, communities, and the world: *Taste-Berry Tales* gives us a glimpse!"
Gayle Wilson, first lady of California

"Bettie Youngs is a grand communicator with an extraordinary gift to write from a place deep within the heart. She understands the authentic tidings of our heartaches and shows us the pot of gold, the butterfly, the new—and truer—self that emerges when we see our lives from possibility, goodness and generosity. These special stories will touch your heart, cause you to think, and stir your soul."
Jane Withers, actress and humanitarian

"I received two of Bettie's books for my birthday and was delighted! Her books should be read by *everyone* as inspiration."
Glenda Eclio, congresswoman, Surigao, Philippines

"As always with Bettie's writings, I find that my heart is deeply stirred by her ability to describe the nobility of the human spirit and our potential to strive for and attain the highest of principled values. In this book of beautiful short stories, Bettie helps us see the importance of helping and supporting others that they, too, might set a moral compass that points in the direction of their finest aspirations."
Sandra Osborn, director of development, Casa De Amparo

"*Taste-Berry Tales* is a source of reminiscent inspiration to me, both professionally and personally. As I write this, I'm preparing to leave for Jamaica to escort a child needing medical care to the Boston hospital. My passionate involvement with Airline Ambassadors' humanitarian aid, blended with countless hours in flight, has afforded me abundant life experiences and rich connections with people. Bettie's inspirational writings reinforce how very precious are the gifts of life and relationship on this planet. They provide a steadfast, guiding source of refreshment, rejuvenation and reassurance in our value to one another and life."
Leeanne Hansen, American Airlines regional director,
Airline Ambassadors International

"Bettie Youngs has an elevated way of seeing the spiritual truth in the ordinary and making it an extraordinary and illuminating experience for her readers. Through the magic of the 'taste-berry consciousness,' daily life becomes a rich classroom for the awakening soul. The stories in this very loving book show us how to open our eyes by looking through the heart and seeing the good around us. This is how the heart and soul are fueled."
Reverend Christian Sorenson, author,
Catch the Spirit: Riding the Waves of Life

"I am enchanted by the soul of this book and by its ability to speak volumes about our times, disclosing both the drama and the simplicity of mankind's inner and outer search for meaning, purpose and direction. As eloquently evidenced by real-life people in these stories, Dr. Youngs shows us there is no mediocrity of soul, and that each life is omnipotently important—and when we treat each other accordingly, we become the taste berry we were intended to be for each other."

P. Juan Armando Perez Talamantes, priest, Monterrey, N. L. Mexico

"It is so inspiring to read the wonderful life-affirming stories in Bettie Youngs's book *Taste-Berry Tales.* How rewarding and reassuring it is to find a kindred soul. My films are all about the family of man and how we are all connected, and so are her stories. In these remarkable tales there is a vision of hope. Through reaching out to our fellow man, our lives are enriched beyond measure. These poignant stories illustrate so vividly the power that a simple, selfless gesture of love can have, and how that cycle of love and caring reaches out and affects us all. This book gives our souls a transfusion of hope, and lights a lamp in a dark and cynical world."

Mark Miller, screenwriter, *Savannah Smiles, A Walk in the Clouds* and *The Shepherd's Song*

"Bettie's soul sings. Her message touches all senses, tendering emotions of affection, sense of color, fragrance and love, giving voice to the intangibles in tangible ways. The result is an enlarged appreciation for life—and seeing more clearly the effects of our trusting the good in others."

Margaret Burke, literary chairman, Round Table West

"Very often in our lives we are asked to cope with extraordinary challenges: our loved ones or we fall sick or suffer injury. What is so particularly important, needed and heartening about *Taste-Berry Tales* is that it reminds us that our thoughtfulness and helpfulness alleviate the suffering of others."

D. J. Mascarenhas, Mumbai, India

"Sometimes it is difficult to tell a leader from a person who is merely 'dressed for success,' or talking the loudest. But as Bettie points out in *Taste-Berry Tales,* we are not running out of good guys—those whose informed, impassioned and integrity-laden guidance always was and always will be important to helping us win at the game of life. This is a book of real-life heroes—'taste berries,' as Bettie calls them—reminding us to cheer for those whose actions are focused on correct principles."

Terry Bradshaw, Hall-of-Fame quarterback, broadcaster and author, *Looking Deep*

"That life is full of trials can be purposeful, opening our hearts, deepening our spirits and connecting us to our higher selves. To that end, we become our own taste berries. What an important outcome. But it can also bring us closer to others, allowing them to help us transform the bitter into the sweet. What a spectacular outcome! This book is a resplendent and delicious treat for the heart."

Tian Dayton, Ph.D., author, *Heartwounds*

"*Taste-Berry Tales* demonstrates a time-honored principle in action: Interdependence is the most purposeful direction of all our efforts. We are each our brother's keeper. This book will warm your heart. Let it be your purpose guide."

Ken Blanchard, coauthor, *The One-Minute Manager*

"What a wonderful concept the taste berry is! That each of us can affect another living entity in a positive way is a loving responsibility we all share. Immediately what comes to mind is my good friend Tippi Hedren and her founding of Shambala to offer a safe and protective environment for big cats. As Bettie Young's story of Subira in this delightful book shows, taste-berry actions such as Tippi's have a ripple effect—continuing to flavor in tangible ways the lives of all those they touch. I love this book—and you will, too."

Betty White, actress and author

"At the heart of each story in *Taste-Berry Tales* lies a parable, a guiding force through which we are nurtured with a spirit of love, of power and of self-efficacy. Our connections with our brothers and sisters transcend the realm of coincidence to that of divine order, and we learn that at the height of our limitations is the strength of our love."

Colleen Morey, Greenwich Public Schools program coordinator: health, physical education, family and consumer sciences

"I can tell you from first-hand experience that Bettie Youngs expands horizons and influences the lives of many people. Her books provide a message that makes communication possible between all people and all things."

Wayne Nishek, Peace Corps country director, Gambia

"In this inspiring book of short stories, Bettie brilliantly uses the taste berry as a metaphor to teach a timeless truth: By helping others find the goodness in their lives—even when our own seem bleak—we lift our own spirits, making our world more manageable through familiarity with theirs. This is the real power of the short story: It is an unparalleled teaching tool for revealing the lesson in virtually any situation or circumstance, such as in her story of the American who befriends a kitty in Manila, and, as a result, his life is transformed. *Taste-Berry Tales* is an elegant book by an eloquent and master storyteller."

Dan Clark, author, *Puppies for Sale and Other Inspirational Tales*

"*Taste-Berry Tales* is a quintessential book, responding to one of the greatest commandments on love: 'Love one another as I have loved you.' *Taste-Berry Tales* unlocks the human goodness in us all. I highly recommend this book: it teaches and gives insight on how to live a life with

meaning and put meaning in our lives."
Brother Mark Kammerer, O.S.B., St. Louis Abbey, St. Louis, Missouri

"Everyone has experienced the lingering warmth of an unexpectedly shown kindness. *Taste-Berry Tales* provides a reserve of that feeling to be portioned out again at the reader's choosing—and, in turn, to be lovingly served to others."

Jane Schorer Meisner, writer and winner,
1991 Pulitzer Prize for public service

"Never before have I been more moved than I was by reading *Taste-Berry Tales*. Bettie finds a way to deliver the 'want to' to her readers that makes them not only think about helping others, but actually gets them out doing it! We need more of this."

Carol Richardson, College of Business and Public Affairs,
Clemson University

"Anyone who has followed Bettie Youngs's writing in the past several years is watching a very special gift unfold. In *Taste-Berry Tales*, Bettie parades her brilliant understanding of life, poignantly and passionately writing from the heart. She has a remarkable understanding of the visible invisibles and makes the invisible visible: quality, character, mood and style all come to life in her hand. Perhaps it's because in both her personal and professional life she walks her talk. Read and savor the ideals expressed in this passionate book."

Jim Cathcart, former president, NSA and author, *The Acorn Principle*

"To Bettie, even the oddities of human character are food for the heart and soul, even the failures of our loving are a way to experience growth and revitalization. Bettie's desire to articulate this duplicity as cherished rather than detrimental is brilliantly accomplished—and gives this book substance, value and merit."

Wayne Dyer, *New York Times* bestselling author

"How can we lift the human spirit and feed the soul? Looking beyond ourselves is the answer *Taste-Berry Tales* embraces. As these stories so vividly illustrate, the only love we get to keep is that which we give away. Read this wonderful book. It will renew your faith in people."

Gloria Lane, founder and president, Women's International Center

"A habit of helping others may be as important to your health and longevity as regular exercise and good nutrition—and offers value to the health of your community and the world as well. In *Taste-Berry Tales*, Bettie illustrates how helping others can move us from the gridlock of our own self-centeredness, and from family, career and financial worries and stress. *Taste-Berry Tales* is just what the doctor ordered."

Harold Bloomfield, M.D., *New York Times* bestselling author,
Hypericum and Depression

"This book is special because Bettie leads the hearts of readers toward positive intentions. Because of it we can see the importance of a happy,

healthy spirit and its contribution to living life in a purposeful way. "
Sara Guntin, educator, Entre Rios, Argentina

"Walking in space is an experience I will never forget. From space, the Earth looks like a tiny blue marble floating in an endless black ocean. The Earth appears so fragile, and yet it is our home, one that supports and sustains so many lives. When gazing at Earth from space, it is impossible to fathom that in communities around the world people are fighting and hurting each other—the idea that we inhabitants of Earth are not cautiously caring for each other and every detail of our environment becomes unbelievable. Looking out for each other and our home planet, paying attention to the details of our environment—things that may seem small and inconsequential, but in the larger scheme of things are vital to a healthy Earth and a healthy, loving global community—are what we all must take to heart . . . and live every day of our lives."
Steve Smith, astronaut

"Once again Bettie puts our lives under scrutiny with her candid eye, penetrating our hearts with her words, all the while coaxing us to come along for a destined journey. *Taste-Berry Tales* melts away our walls and barriers to reveal to us a tranquil yet durable core. An excellent read."
Karen Holt, Gannett News

"*Taste-Berry Tales* is an important and priceless book about restoring our trust in others. Even more so, it's a wakeup call, asking us to envision a better world. We can all use seeing a bit differently. Goodness, like charity and kindness, is a necessary perspective, and much needed in today's times. Read this book, and give it as a gift. Let it find a home in your heart, and become a tool to change someone else's."
Mort Crim, broadcaster and author, *Second Thoughts*

"Always I am touched by the human warmth and compassion of Bettie's books, and their ability to touch hearts. When I read *Values from the Heartland,* I felt as if she had visited my soul, or at the very least was speaking directly to it. *Taste-Berry Tales* does that in spades."
Analisa Eterno, Manila, Philippines

"I enjoyed Dr. Youngs new book immensely. Although I was already familiar with her writing from using one of her earlier books, *You and Self-Esteem,* with my daughter, I got even more out of this book because of the uncanny way she has of using stories to make her point. We do that often in Russia, so to see that technique used so effectively means to me that this book will be of value in my country as well as in other lands around the world that are used to using stories to enhance the learning and healing process between people."
Oleg. Y. Tchernoskutov, president, Puls Technology and publisher, Moscow, Russia

Taste-Berry™
Tales

STORIES TO LIFT THE SPIRIT, FILL THE HEART AND FEED THE SOUL

Bettie B. Youngs, Ph.D., Ed.D.

Health Communications, Inc.
Deerfield Beach, Florida

www.hci-online.com

Library of Congress Cataloging-in-Publication Data

Youngs, Bettie B., date.
    Taste-berry tales: stories to lift the spirit, fill the heart, and feed the soul/
    Bettie B. Youngs.
        p.   cm.
    ISBN 1-55874-548-3. — ISBN 1-55874-547-5 (pbk.)
    1. Conduct of life.   I. Title.
    BJ1597.Y68   1998   97-50414
    170'.44—dc21   CIP

©1998 Bettie B. Youngs
ISBN 1-55874-547-5 trade paper
ISBN 1-55874-548-3 hardcover

Publisher: Health Communications, Inc.
             3201 S.W. 15th Street
             Deerfield Beach, Florida 33442-8190

Cover illustration and design by Andrea Perrine Brower

To know that even one life has
breathed easier because you have lived—
this is to have succeeded.

—Ralph Waldo Emerson

This book is dedicated to those
who help us see from the eyes of the heart,
a perspective making clear that it is our honor
—as much as it is our obligation—to assist
others to "breath easier," to see their
lives as precious, full of hope, less
impossible and more glorious.

Also by Bettie B. Youngs

Gifts of the Heart: Stories That Celebrate Life's Defining Moments (Health Communications, Inc.)

Values from the Heartland (Health Communications, Inc.)

Stress & Your Child: Helping Kids Cope with the Strains & Pressures of Life (Random House)

Safeguarding Your Teenager from the Dragons of Life: A Guide to the Adolescent Years (Health Communications, Inc.)

How to Develop Self-Esteem in Your Child: 6 Vital Ingredients (Macmillan/Ballantine)

Self-Esteem for Educators: It's Job Criteria #1 (Jalmar Press)

Keeping Our Children Safe: A Guide to Emotional, Physical, Intellectual and Spiritual Wellness (John Knox/Westminster Press)

You and Self-Esteem: A Book for Young People (Jalmar Press)

Developing Self-Esteem in Your Students: A K-12 Curriculum (Jalmar Press)

Getting Back Together: Repairing Love (Adams Media Corp.)

Is Your Net-Working? A Complete Guide to Building Contacts and Career Visibility (John Wiley)

Managing Your Response to Stress: A Guide for Administrators (Jalmar Press)

Contents

Acknowledgments

Regardless of who we are or what we do for work or play, a common mission for each of us is to earn respect for the intricate gift of life—our own, and that which exists all around us. We are given an infinite array of experiences to learn that it is our daily obligation and responsibility, as much as it is our honor, to see our lives in the most positive light. Luckily, all around us are people who, in their acceptance of us as well as their refusal to accept the parts of us they know we really didn't choose, cause us to become better than we might have been without them. They are true taste berries, making our lives sweeter.

In that vein, I'd like to thank some taste berries in the development of this book. First and foremost I must return a heart of love to Ron Kallem (and his taste berry, Zelda) for crystallizing the theme of this book, and for their generous time and love to my family. To my publishers Peter Vegso and Gary Seidler and the talented staff at Health Communications, most especially to editors Matthew Diener, Christine Belleris, Lisa Drucker and Erica Orloff; and to Andrea Perrine Brower for the beautiful cover design, a heartfelt thanks. All paved the way to bring the mission of this book to life, as did Debra Leone and Tina Moreno of my staff; a very special thanks for their work on this book.

To the taste berries in my personal life, most especially those who are my anchors in all times: my daughter Jennifer and her father, Dic Youngs; my parents, Arlene and Everett Burres; and my brothers and sisters. And to a "perfectly good

Texas boy," my husband David, a man of extraordinary wisdom, compassion and love. Their contributions to my life are deeply grasped and much honored.

Introduction

I've been thinking about the duplicity of the messages that are a part of our times and considering their effects on our lives. We are taught, for example, to value and hold in high esteem the morals of the stories about the survival of the fittest, the victory of the strongest, the success of the shrewdest. These are considered "winners" in our society. And yet, the same aggressive personality honored on the sports field can prove fatal at home. The same board of directors that makes decisions to fund charitable community projects may also make decisions that can ultimately wreck communities, ruin families and despoil nature. Precious little is said about (or credence given to) the eminence of the most honest, the most serving, the most giving, the most loving. So we strive to be the strongest, the toughest, the most clever—in one way or another—as if to be any less is to be inadequate or deemed a loser.

Taking note of the dynamic times in which I live, I realize I'm part of a generation in which all the rules have been questioned, and many have been rewritten: Quantity is used in the same breath as quality; image is considered as much of the equation for success as integrity; independence is assigned as much value as interdependence (codependence and dysfunction are virtually interchangeable words); rebellion is as honored as harmony; promises, like appointments, are frequently broken; long-term goals are sacrificed for immediate results; truth is altered in the name of greed, expediency or convenience.

What detrimental trade-offs these turn out to be. Many fears now abound—so many that we question whether it's safe for us to stop at the side of a road and assist a pregnant woman holding a young child and standing next to a car with a flat tire! We live in a world of changing values, shifting mores, clashing dissonance and, unfortunately, newscasts that are more likely to fill the airwaves with stories of humanity at its lowest and worst rather than its achievements and good deeds. As Chris Burke said to me, "Read the sports page first. It's filled with mankind's victories; the front page is filled with our defeats."

Ours is a time in which we honor and set up as a role model the most bellicose character, yet fail to hail the person who devotes selfless and tireless time, guidance and direction to caretaking and caregiving roles—such as a parent, teacher, volunteer or community activist. It's a time when fast-talking, silver-tongued motivational speakers champion various versions of the "dress for success" and "unlimited power" themes; one in which infomercial gurus insidiously try to convince us to buy their latest quick fix for a better life—everything from a psychic hotline to spray-on hair.

While some of these measures can prove useful, something is missing in these frantic messages, something far more important for which we should strive. I wonder if an overemphasis on "up the corporate ladder," a focus on having and getting (at the expense of being and becoming), looking out for number one, and quick fixes aren't in direct opposition to the human spirit. Most especially, I wonder if they are in opposition to deepening into life, that is, honoring and living the purpose of our existence. To me, the invisible visibles—the growing complaints of absence of quality, mood, style and spirit—speak volumes. They are all signs of something deeper: Though in cosmic harmony, many hearts are in lonely exile.

Can we withstand the constant image of ourselves being, in basketball star Dennis Rodman's words, "as bad as I wanna be"? Is the constant barrage of this message good for us? Is the continual reflection of mankind without morals—dangerous, deadly people lacking pity, empathy or remorse, which is commonly the stuff of horror films, sensational trials, shrill tabloid media hype and draconian political action by "tough on crime" legislators—really the way we are? Or does it just seem so? Isn't the impression, as so many young people seem to have, that one must "get the other guy before he gets you" suffocating the human spirit? Year after year, crime after crime, we feel the pain of such actions. We are constantly reminded that the environments we create are not entirely our own. We believe that a growing distrust of others, a constant media-inspired fear of being victimized and individual powerlessness are the price we must pay for living in modern society.

I think it's morally toxic, and a terrible debilitating curse, to believe that imperfect role models—false gods of material success and shallow fame—have taken over. Though their influence is magnified by the vast capability of the media today, we do not live in a world where individuals are preoccupied with what is owed them rather than what they owe to others, where they place blame rather than accept responsibility. It is, as President Bill Clinton said recently, "the struggle we face today, in a world more high-tech, more fast-moving, more chaotically diverse than ever, the age-old fight between hope and fear."

We must choose hope over fear.

Are we a thoughtless, self-centered, uncaring people? Or do we just not hear about the times when we are actively involved with others? Prince Michael of Greece quickly discovered this other view during an interview with Mother Teresa when he told her, "There may be hope in the streets of Calcutta, but there is little or none in the streets of New York."

"Oh, no!" Mother Teresa burst out defiantly. "That can't be! There are many people ready and willing to help." I want to believe as Mother Teresa did, that we can and do reach out to each other by helping, supporting, assisting—being "our brother's keeper." It matters that we do. If we can set a moral compass that points in the direction of our finest aspirations, we can achieve what we all want without diminishing our neighbor's share. Examples are all around us.

A friend and I had just returned from visiting Tippi Hedren in Southern California. Ms. Hedren has crafted Shambala, a beautiful ranch in Soledad Canyon providing a safe and loving shelter for abandoned and abused big cats. Those who visit often come away with new insights relevant to their own lives. Memorable on my last visit was Subira, a cheetah born with a defect, an imperfect animal born into an insecure world that sets up perfection as a standard for acceptance. Imperfection, as Subira learned, could trigger an order for her death. Cast out from a world-famous zoo that was to be her showcase, she now resides at Shambala. Subira has become an example of hope and light: Because of her, hundreds of people each year open to victory over their own challenges.

Fresh on my hands are abrasions from assisting Habitat for Humanity (an international nonprofit housing ministry that builds and rehabilitates homes for families in need) cofounder Linda Caldwell Fuller in a "blitz" build. Volunteers—skilled and unskilled, young and old, and from every walk of life— gathered from around the globe to work side-by-side, shoulder-to-shoulder, building a home for the Marez family in Cathedral City. And there's the kitty from Manila who felt so cheated out of love that when she finally found someone to provide it— even a stranger—she allowed herself to slip peacefully beyond the last of her nine lives. This incident was so poignant for her caretaker that it became a paradigm shift allowing him to forge a new direction in his life.

Still stirring around in my soul are the heart-wrenching stories I listened to while I was a guest on the *Geraldo Rivera* show. Assembled was a panel of mothers, fathers and young people victimized by senseless highway shootings. These reports were so harrowing that even though I was serving in the role of guest expert on the show, I was silenced. Yet, individual family members rose above their despair, like the Phoenix rising from the ashes, to work tirelessly for the safety of others by initiating local, state and national reform, even though it was too late for their own loved ones to benefit. Another panel member, Jimmy Mitchell, a Good Samaritan who stopped to help an injured motorist, was left paralyzed from his gunshot wounds. An entire community opened their hearts, as well as their wallets to help him cope with his disabilities.

And what of Mother Teresa, an "old woman," as she called herself, who began her mission in 1952 by picking up one dying man from a sewer in Calcutta, providing love and comfort in his final days? In the next thirty years, she and her sisters in the Missionaries of Charity picked up over 40,000 dying people. The fact that nearly half have recovered is a remarkable testimony to the healing power of love. And her legacy lives on.

These stories and the people they are about highlight how much we are needed by each other. Their compassionate gestures are a road map to feeding our spirits, hearts and souls.

These were among the things I mulled over as I returned to my hometown this past Thanksgiving for a visit with family and friends. As I attended a church service with them one Sunday, I was pleasantly surprised to see a former high school classmate and friend, Ron Kallem, sitting in the front pew with his wife, Zelda. I hadn't seen Ron since he was employed in the same city where I lived, at the same radio station where, coincidentally, my then-fiancée worked (this was nearly ten years after our high school days together). Another decade had passed since those days in radio, and here he was that day. Ron was more than a member of the congregation, however: He was pastor of this church!

Not only was it good to see Ron again, but it was such interesting timing: Pastor Ron, as he is affectionately called, approached the pulpit and delivered a sermon that held up faith as the Christian's taste berry. Pastor Ron said, "Sorrowing heart, burdened soul, disappointed or lonely spirit: For the Christian, faith in God takes the sting out of the experience. We are called upon to do nothing less. We are all interrelated and interdependent: We are each our brother's keeper. We need each other, sometimes in the role of a taste berry."

A taste berry?

There is a fruit called the Richardella-dulcisica, better known as the "taste berry." When eaten, the taste buds experience whatever is being consumed—even distasteful foodstuffs—as sweet and delicious. Aboriginal tribes often use the taste berry as a way of tolerating—even enjoying—things in their diet that they may not be able to consume otherwise.

Just as faith is the taste berry for Christians, Tippi Hedren is for the cats of Shambala; Millard Fuller, Linda Caldwell Fuller, Jimmy Carter and Rosalynn Carter are for hundreds of families who now have shelter; Subira is for Cory; the American is for Manila Kitty; the citizens of Wabash, Indiana, are for Jimmy Mitchell; Mother Teresa's legacy, offering love and understanding without judgment, is to those her charity still serves; and those who work to make our communities safer—even though their own loved ones will no longer benefit from such measures—are for all of us. We all need taste berries. Just as the infant needs physical touch in order to survive, we all—young and old alike—need fuel to nourish a sense of goodness. Not to merely look through the lens of rose-colored glasses, but rather, to see the good of an experience and allow it to flavor our lives. Without taste berries, we may come to believe that life is sour, that we are sour; but we are not. By seeing through the eyes of goodness, we can lift our spirits, feed our souls and nourish our hearts— and our health.

An interesting study was conducted by Harvard professor Dr. David McClelland regarding the crucial roles of giving and receiving love (termed *affiliative trust*) in healing and overall well-being. Participants in the study were asked to watch a documentary on the life of Mother Teresa or short clips of others who helped or acted in a kind manner to another. The results of the tests given in this well-documented study revealed two significant findings. First, because they were so motivated by what they saw, participants expressed an overwhelming desire to "get involved in doing something positive." Secondly, an antibody found in the saliva of those in the study (secretory immunoglobulin, s-IsA for short) rose significantly. This antibody is the first line of defense against germs that enter through the nose and mouth, and is an integral part of the body's defense against infectious disease. Moreover, when each participant was asked to close her eyes and recall a time from her own life when she was either giving (caregiving) or receiving unconditional love, once again her body experienced a significant increase in s-IsA. People have a greater propensity to heal—and reach a higher level of health, happiness and creativity—when they feel a positive interdependence with others.

What is lost in so many lives—and must be recovered—is

the trust that others will each reach out in safe ways to help, support and assist. This is a book of real-life "taste berries." I hope that the stories in this book, and the people you'll meet through them, help you see our world as full of hope, less impossible and more glorious. May the experience of the goodness of these individuals find a home in your heart and mind, and add to your sense of compassion for others.

While reading these stories, I encourage you to pay particular attention to the common themes that bind them together— the deep sense of connection, belonging and gratitude, and a renewed sense that we are all fellow travelers, each tied to a larger sense of humanity. We are connected. Sometimes it takes another—be it a child, parent, educator, spouse, coworker, grandpa, angel or pet—to help us open to life, to greet and meet the challenges found there. This does not take away from the idea that we each are responsible for our own lives and the way we live them. Nor does it lessen the notion that in each of our lives there is an individual plan, uniquely ours, for fulfill-ment—one that only we can experience as we do. It's just that sometimes when our own inner wisdom knocks at our door, we send it away because we are afraid or lack courage to do what it's asking us to do. Sometimes all it takes is a loving action from another to remind us, guide us and encourage us to trust our own inner voice, the one that sets the course, steers the ship and guides the journey.

Lastly, may we each become a taste berry for another. Looking at our fellow travelers through the eyes of the heart can remind us that we are all soul journeyers. There is no such thing as a mediocre soul, only each of us trying to make our way on the journey. By supporting and assisting each other along the way, the journey can be sweeter.

1 What $300 Can Buy

Allan is a friend of mine. A good friend. Even so, he's the kind of person that you can tolerate only so long before he gets on your nerves. But on his birthday, I called him as I do every year.

"Happy birthday, Allan!" I chirped when he answered his phone.

"Right," he replied bleakly. "What can be *happy* about turning fifty? With my luck, the cost of my life insurance will go up!"

"Let me take you out for dinner," I suggested.

"Do I have to wear a suit?" he moaned.

"No," I replied. "Slacks and a great sports coat will be fine."

"Well, okay then," he conceded.

I took him to a nice Italian restaurant, one of his few favorites. I'd arranged for the waiters to present a cupcake with a candle in the center to Allan and sing "Happy Birthday" to him after dinner.

"Oh, Lord!" Allan said, rolling his eyes and squirming in his chair as they sang. "How long will they go on?" Though he tried not to look self-conscious, he was thoroughly annoyed. It was great fun watching!

"The 'Happy Birthday' song is usually pretty short," I informed him, really enjoying all this. "And I've asked them to sing it through only three times."

When the birthday choir left the table, I presented my friend with a gift, a simple, safe-to-give-to-any-man present.

"Bloomingdale's?" he screeched when he saw the store's customary wrapping with its name emblazoned on it. "You bought it at Bloomingdale's?" Fumbling with the wrapping paper, he added, "I know this cost an arm and a leg." The instant he saw that it was a designer sweatshirt, he ordered, "You've got to take it back. You know they've marked this thing up twenty times more than it's worth!"

"If you don't like it or if it doesn't fit, exchange it," I instructed. Looking him directly in the eyes, I ordered, "Under no circumstances are you to take it back and hand me a store credit in my name—as you did with the last birthday gift I bought you!"

"I like the sweatshirts I buy at Wal-Mart," he retorted.

"You can buy a good sweatshirt for $15 or less at Wal-Mart. Why spend more?"

Allan is so Allan.

I met him at a social gathering twenty years ago, right around the time he started a business manufacturing floppy diskettes for the computer industry. Eventually, the tiny little company he began in his office at home moved into his garage, and then took over an entire five-story office building. Five years ago, he sold the company for $35 million, retaining the division that manufactured replacement parts. This he did so that, in his words, he'd "have an income, and something to do."

As well as being wealthy, Allan is very handsome and, though extremely shy, he's a friendly sort of fellow, very likable. He has never married but would like nothing more. "I'm rich and good looking," he candidly remarked to me last year, "but I've only had four dates in the last five years. What is so wrong with me that I can't find someone to love?"

Unfortunately, he counts pennies as if his present or immediate future faced financial devastation. He never plays with carefree abandon, nor relaxes in a spirit of leisure. He doesn't give, doesn't spend, doesn't seem to enjoy life.

Maybe it's one of the reasons he's had four dates in five years.

Allan called a week later to say thanks for the birthday dinner and gift, and to tell me that, yes, he had taken the sweatshirt back and a gift certificate was being mailed to me in my name. What I said to him may have been because of what he did, or maybe it was just the extra long week I'd had. Or maybe it was because, as I listened to Allan complain and complain, I was put off by all the negativity. "Allan," I said in exasperation, "you know I'm your friend, and you know I'd do anything for you, but really, your woebegone attitude is getting very old. All you do is focus on how miserable you are. Pardon my saying so, but I think your 'poor me' shtick is very selfish. I'm going to make a suggestion. I know this is going to be a major undertaking for you, but I'm going to suggest it anyway. Tomorrow, take three $100 bills and go to that grocery store that's near your house. Walk down several aisles observing the other people in the store as you walk. The moment you see a woman with several children, one you know has more bills than she can comfortably meet, walk up to her and, without saying anything other than 'I hope you have a great day, ma'am,' hand her one of those $100 bills. Then smile and walk away. Just so long as you give it to a mother with a group of children.

"Then, walk up and down the aisle until you come to a senior citizen carefully reading and comparing the cost of two items, trying to decide which one is cheaper because he or she is obviously on a strict budget. I want you to take the second $100 bill and give it to him, again just saying something like 'It's your lucky day. This is for you, spend it as you wish.' And once again, turn and walk away.

"Spend the last $100 bill on yourself. Buy yourself something without fretting over the possibility that if you hunted long enough and hard enough you might have found it somewhere else for less. Something you really like.

I suggest a body massage, a facial and a pedicure. I think if you follow those instructions you'll find at least a glimmer in the right direction for snapping out of your depression." These were not the words Allan wanted to hear. "What?" Allan roared, his tone indicating he thought I'd gone mad. "*Why* would I do that? I have to go now. I feel *worse* than when I called." With that, he hung up.

I thought I might not hear from him again.

Two months later, I answered my doorbell to find Allan standing on my doorstep. Grinning from ear to ear, he announced, "I did it! I spent the $300 as you suggested. Care to hear about it?"

"Absolutely!" I said, inviting him in.

"It was a pretty interesting experience," he explained. His excitement over sharing the story quickly transformed into sincerity and empathy. "You should have seen the look on that mother's face," he said with a look of amazement now on his own. "And the kids that were with her! Five of them no less, and they looked to be under the age of ten— or maybe eight. Somewhere in that age range. I can't imagine what caring for that many small children must be like. My sister has two and it's more than she can handle. Plus, kids—at least my sister's—are very expensive. I mean, it's clothes, $100 tennis shoes, food, and always a hand being held out wanting money for things like movies, the video arcade, new sports equipment.

"And the older man, Philip," he said, moving right along, shaking his head as he chuckled with glee. As though transported back to that encounter in the store's aisle, Allan gazed thoughtfully at the floor as he spoke.

"That was something. He reacted to the $100 as though I was Santa Claus."

"And the last $100?" I questioned.

He held up his wrist proudly displaying a new watch.

"I'm proud of you, Allan," I said.

His face glowing, he said in delight, "I know what you were trying to teach me. I guess I'd gotten myself into a case of chronic self-pity and couldn't ever be happy because I didn't particularly like myself." He wagged his head as he marveled at his own folly.

"Allan," I said, feeling his satisfaction, "I'm genuinely pleased with you." Thinking of the last time we talked, I added, "When I asked you to do this, I was probably out of line, but I was just so frustrated with you. There are so many people who would love to have the opportunities you have and are willing to tolerate the downside of your life in exchange for it. I just felt that you were too wrapped up in yourself, and that maybe if you'd be concerned about another person for a minute, you'd find some happiness." Having tried to explain my logic, I apologized for my lack of patience, "But I am sorry for being short with you."

"Don't be sorry. It was a wonderful lesson," he reported earnestly. "And you know what else I learned?"

"What's that?" I prompted.

"I learned that financial success is empty until it serves a purpose," he stated thoughtfully. Then his face brightened again. "And that it's really great fun having money! You'll never guess what I did after I spent the first $300." My expression coaxed him to go on.

"The day after my big spending spree—" catching himself, his eyes instantly met my eyes and he amended his statement. "Well, okay, my 'little' spending spree—a brochure arrived in the mail from a local animal shelter. It had a heart-wrenching photo of this skinny, malnourished, yet full-of-spirit dog on the cover, with a caption that read, 'Please give me a home.' The picture inspired me to—"

"Let me guess!" I interrupted, laughing at how much fun this "project" had been for him. "You now own a dog!"

"No," he chuckled. "I didn't go that far, but I did visit the shelter. You should see all the dogs and cats—and kittens and puppies—the shelter provides for and houses. I don't understand how people can mistreat defenseless animals. Some of them were sick, undernourished, and most all of them were craving attention. The number of animals that are abandoned every year is unbelievable. The shelter depends on donations to care for them, so when I saw the work they were doing, I mean, it's such a good cause—"

"So you donated to them, too?" I guessed correctly, laughing at the joyful grin on his face as he nodded. "You're on a roll!" I teased. "And look at you! I couldn't be more thrilled to see how happy you are!"

"Thank you for giving me the wake-up call," he said, the look in his eyes growing serious. "It was insightful. Actually, it's changed my life. Most especially the experience with Philip. When I came upon him in the store, because his vision was so bad, he was holding a can really close to his face trying to read the label on the can. He had cataracts and was darn near blind because of them. When Philip told me that he didn't have a driver's license because of the loss of his sight, I offered him a ride home. You should have seen the terrible place he lived in—an old tattered shanty of a trailer. As we arrived, he apologized for the way the place looked, explaining that retirement had been more expensive than he'd imagined, and then his wife had ongoing health problems that added up to huge medical bills—which their insurance only covered partially. It was obvious he had no money, though he'd once had a successful little franchise, a copy-center place. I never used it, but I do remember it. It was on the corner where that new hotel sits."

"Is his wife well now?" I asked.

"No," Allan responded softly. "He lost Beth just three years ago."

I took note of the fact that Allan had taken Philip to heart. Obviously they had more than a passing conversation. He knew of Beth and felt deeply for Philip.

"It seems that with every passing year life gets worse for Philip," Allan said. "And though money isn't the answer to all of his problems, it can go a long way toward fixing some of them—like his eyesight for instance. I found out that without cataract surgery Philip's eyesight would deteriorate to the point of not being able to see at all. So I contacted a good friend, Dr. Lee Nordan, an excellent eye surgeon, and asked him to evaluate Philip's health and ability to undergo surgery. Well, Philip was a good candidate, so first we did his right eye, and four weeks later we did his left eye."

"*We?*" I questioned.

"Well, Lee did the surgery, but you know," he shrugged modestly, "I covered the bill."

"How wonderful for Philip," I said, duly impressed.

"Yes, it really is," Allan admitted. "And not just for him, but for me, too."

It was from this vantage point that I noticed Allan's great-looking boots.

"Nice boots!" I commented.

"Oh, thanks," he said. "Philip was wearing an old pair of nice-looking boots, and when I mentioned that I liked the style, he told me that some fifteen years ago he'd had them made for him. I thought, *What a great idea.*" Laughing playfully he said, "So, I ordered a pair custom made just for me." He looked down at the fine leather cowboy boots he sported, then hopped to his feet to model them with a cocky smile, saying, "It's amazing what $300 can buy!" He grew thoughtful and added, "In the process of spending the $300, I learned to like myself. Giving is about appreciating. One benefit of having money is for stuff like this," he said, pointing to his boots, "and also to use for *others.* It's been a long time—if there ever was a time—since I enjoyed myself more than I did assisting Philip to have better vision and a better life or even the mother in the store, though a hundred dollars won't go very far with growing children. Thanks for leading me to the experience. I needed it. It was a godsend, really. Now, do you know any great women?" he asked lightheartedly. "I'd sure like to meet the *right* woman!"

What Allan didn't tell me, but what I later learned, was that when Philip came home from the recovery center after his second cataract operation, it was a new, though modest, trailer home that he came home to—courtesy of Allan!

Allan took Philip to heart—to his heart—and in his heart found compassion for Philip's predicament. This in turn ignited Allan's desire to share and to help others. He became a taste berry for Philip, and because of it discovered one ingredient of the happiness for which he hungered: giving of himself.

As Allan said, "It's amazing what $300 can buy."

2

Special #2, Please

It had been a late night. My flight arrived in San Diego right around midnight, and by the time I drove home and got into bed it was nearly 2:00 A.M. I was still in need of sleep and jet-lagged from being on East Coast time when I stumbled out of bed the next day. Nevertheless, I had to be up bright and early that morning: I was the 9:00 A.M. opening keynoter at a national conference.

In short, I needed to recover quickly. *A hearty breakfast in the early morning sun is what I need,* I decided. I quickly showered, dressed, collected my briefcase and papers, and headed to Carlos & Annie's, a popular restaurant located in the heart of the seaside town of Del Mar, California—the perfect little nook of quaint Spanish colonial charm.

Waiting patiently for a parking spot in the crowded lot near the restaurant, I watched the hand of my watch as minutes ticked away. When the car I was waiting on finally vacated its space, a man rudely zipped his car into *my* parking space. Seething in frustrated silence, I drove on and looked for another place to park.

"I'd like steak and eggs, please," I said to the waitress after I had at last found another place to park and a table in the restaurant. "And a serious orange juice."

"Oh, I'm sorry," she apologized. "We're out of Special #2. We've served the last of our steaks. But we have—"

I'm not sure if it was my heartfelt moan that caught Carlos the owner's attention as he sauntered from the restaurant's kitchen to the outdoor patio where I was seated or if his watchful eye had glimpsed my distress. With a smile on his face and his hands in his pockets, Carlos came striding over and listened attentively to our exchange.

"Oh, I don't just *want* steak and eggs," I groaned. "You know how sometimes you just *need* steak and eggs?"

The lovely young waitress smiled and then laughed. "Yes," she admitted, "I do! So, then, how about Special #14, Carlos & Annie's famous biscuits and gravy, or maybe #10, a dish of huevos rancheros. It's really popular with the 'It's so early, I'm so tired but I still gotta work' crowd!"

"Oh, no steak and eggs?" I couldn't seem to accept it.

Carlos studied me for a moment. His warm, caring brown eyes seemed intent on pinpointing the best solution.

Then, a wide smile stretching beneath his bushy salt-and-pepper mustache, he said, "You know, I think I did see one final steak back there."

Pressing my luck, I quickly declared, "Wow, that would be great. But you know, I'm not sure if I want a breakfast steak at all. What I really want is a steak—you know, one that's two inches thick, tender and juicy, with next to no marbling, served medium rare. That's what I *really* want." While my first words were said with dreamy enthusiasm, my final words were forlorn and came a split second before I realized that I had all but said "no" to the one and only little breakfast steak remaining in the kitchen.

"Not to worry," Carlos assured me, adjusting his turquoise bolo tie at the collar of his plaid denim shirt and hitching up his black denim pants. He tipped his wide-brimmed gray cowboy hat with a wink and said, "I have just what the doctor ordered." He turned around and headed toward the kitchen, his ostrich boots clicking across the Spanish tile.

The young waitress gave me a wink as well and said with a knowing smile, "Carlos is being Carlos again!"

At the time, I was too groggy to give her statement much thought.

Carlos didn't stay in the kitchen at all. As I sat there sipping my juice, I glimpsed Carlos as he left the restaurant through the side door. With both hands in his pockets, he walked briskly across the street and into a cozy neighborhood grocery store. Within minutes, he emerged from the store with a sack in his hand. As he strode back toward the restaurant, he was slowed first by Jenny Hawkins, a local attorney on her way to her office, then by Tom Richie, branch sales manager for Coldwell Banker and the chamber of commerce president, and finally by former mayor and real estate developer Tom Pearson on his way to his office. Carlos stopped briefly with each of them. He patted Tom Richie on the shoulder and exchanged morning greetings with Jenny Hawkins and Tom Pearson. He waved congenially to still others—all while hurrying back to the restaurant. Before reentering the restaurant, he stopped one final time to help Anne Mery, the proprietor of the Earth Song bookstore next door by holding the items that filled her arms so she could search her large crowded key ring for the key to the door.

Within minutes after he left the restaurant, my waitress stepped out of the kitchen, carrying a plate that held eggs and a thick, juicy, two-inch steak!

Several weeks after that incident, I learned that Carlos and his wife Annie had sold their restaurant three weeks *before* the morning of my Special #2. Carlos and Annie had quietly retired and were moving to Santa Fe, New Mexico. With this news came the realization that Carlos hadn't gone to such extra lengths for me simply because it was "good business" or because I served on the chamber of commerce with him. It was because Special #2s were his *personal* standard.

Carlos's Special #2 is much more than a selection on a menu. Special #2 is about understanding that we are fellow travelers and, even though we are usually wrapped up in our own lives and busy doing our own things, patience, tolerance, courtesy and kindness are called for just the same. Carlos's actions remind us that acts of kindness should not be random, they should be a personal standard.

Carlos pampered me that morning by making certain I had breakfast *exactly* as I wanted it, and his actions buffered my fatigue and offset the annoyance I felt at the man who robbed me of a parking space. But it did so much more. It also served to remind me that while I live in a world where someone would just as soon take *my* parking space as look for his own, I also live in a world where others are helpful and go out of their way on my behalf. Just yesterday, a woman standing in the checkout line at the grocery store—carrying a crying infant in one arm and unloading a cart full of items with the other—upon seeing my haste, asked if I'd like to go in front of her. The post office manager allowed me to slip in even after the "one minute to closing" rule. And the customer service personnel at the department store listened with acceptance even though I went overboard expressing my disappointment with an item that had been incorrectly marked and how inconvenient it was to return it.

Reminding ourselves that we live in a world where people assist each other serves to do something even more: It encourages us to extend our acts of kindness beyond friends and loved ones to others we pass along the way. It also encourages us to be kind and thoughtful—even when someone else may not be.

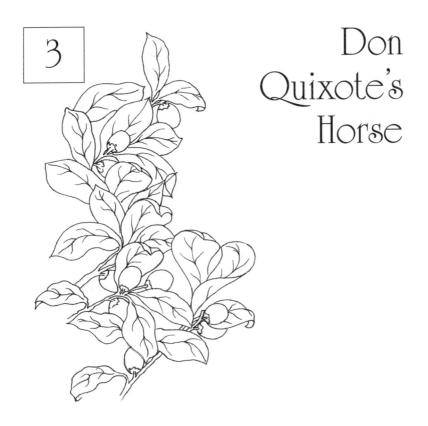

3

Don Quixote's Horse

"It'll *never* happen!" said my good friend Joy when I told her I needed to get in to see Vic Preisser, the commissioner for the Iowa Department of Social Services. "I hear he's a most *difficult* man—a no-nonsense, cantankerous tough guy!"

I'd completed a Ph.D. degree several years earlier, and now I wanted to add an Ed.D. to my credentials, a degree that focused on the principles of leadership, management and supervision. One of the requirements of this doctoral program was to complete separate internships with contemporary leaders in each of three fields: business, education and government. The goal was to examine traits of dynamic and exemplary leadership.

I'd completed my internship in education with Dr. Dick Sweeney, one of the most respected leaders in school leadership in the state. I'd finished my business internship with Joe Batten, a leading management guru in the nation and founder of BBH&S, a consulting firm serving Fortune 500 companies. Only the government internship remained.

In discussing the parameters of this last internship, several members of the university's doctoral committee suggested names of leaders from whom I might acquire an *exemplary* experience. "An internship with Vic Preisser would be an *interesting* experience," grinned Dr. Gable, the head of my program. Instantly, a look of alarm appeared on the faces of several members of the committee. Others smiled and lowered their eyes to the papers before them.

"She'll never get to him," Dr. Alan Watts said candidly.

"That's true," Dr. Erickson confirmed. Perhaps taking pity on me, he made a suggestion: "Maybe Tom Brayden, head of United Way, would be a better choice for her. It might be easier for her to get an interview. The internship has to be completed by springtime." Everyone murmured in agreement. Even so, the decision was up to me. The skeptical responses of the committee members to my securing and completing an internship with Mr. Preisser only served to pique my curiosity and my desire to work with him.

The next day I called Mr. Preisser's office. His receptionist informed me that he was out of town on business and that I should try back in a few days. Several days later I called again. This time the receptionist informed me that he was in town but wasn't accepting calls. Or appointments. I heard the same story the next day. And the next. And every day for two weeks. Since time was running out, I decided I needed to take more action: I'd visit him in person, without an appointment.

When I arrived at Mr. Preisser's office, I discovered that he had not one but three secretaries. Their desks were lined up in a row so that you had to stop and get clearance from one secretary before you could proceed to the next. The desks of the first two secretaries faced in the direction of those approaching his office. The desk closest to Mr. Preisser's office faced his office—with that secretary's back to the other two secretaries.

"Hi, I'm here to see Mr. Preisser," I said, straightening the jacket of my new gray wool business suit.

With a look of complete amusement washing across her face, the first secretary asked casually, "Do you have an appointment?"

"No, but I was hoping—"

"Here's the number if you'd like to call and make an appointment," she said, grinning.

"Why don't I just make one with him now?" I reasoned.

"Okay," she said, picking up the phone and dialing the secretary that sat less than four feet away. Secretary number two picked up her phone when it rang. The two secretaries spoke back and forth while looking at me, primly suppressing condescending giggles. Finally secretary number two—her tone making it clear there was really little hope in it—said, "Tell her he has an opening in five months but to call the week before to confirm."

Upstaged by their antics, I excused myself and huffed away. As soon as I was out the door, I realized I had lost, and their system worked. I still had no appointment. Everyone had been right about Preisser. His system was foolproof. It seemed simply impossible to move beyond the second secretary, much less get in to see Mr. Preisser himself. I looked down at the form in my hand, a contractual agreement that needed to be agreed to and signed by Mr. Preisser before the end of the week.

As I looked up from the contract, I saw Mr. Preisser's first and second secretaries heading to the lunchroom at the same time. Suddenly, the possibility of a solution appeared to me. Taking note of the time, I left the building. I would return to Mr. Preisser's office the next day to try my luck again, only this time I had a "new and improved plan"!

The following day I arrived at the same time I had noted the day before. Just as I had hoped, secretaries number one and number two were not at their desks. I approached secretary number three. "I'd like to see Mr. Preisser," I announced with confidence.

"Do you have an appointment?" the professionally groomed woman asked, her tone one of efficient courtesy. With a puzzled frown she dutifully scanned Mr. Preisser's appointment book, then answered her question for me, "I'm sorry, Mr. Preisser isn't taking appointments today."

"I'd really like to see him," I said as I laid a crisp $100 bill on her desk, a bill I'd obtained at the bank specifically for this moment. "Please tell Mr. Preisser that Dr. Youngs is here to see him and would like to *buy* five minutes of his time."

The stunned woman looked first at me, then at the $100 bill, and then back at me again. Without saying a word, she got up and went into Mr. Preisser's office, closing the door behind her. In nervous anticipation, I waited.

Within moments a huge roar came from the room, the door opened, and a fit, smartly dressed and attractive, six-foot-four-inch man emerged, still belly laughing. "Come on in, then," he chortled. "Have a seat."

I laid the document that outlined my academic agreement on his desk with the expectation of discussing it. Instead, he snatched up the paper before I could say anything, glanced at it momentarily, scrawled his name across the sheet and slid it back across the desk to me. "Okay, so what is it you'd like to talk about?" he asked. Glancing down at his watch, he added, "You still have four minutes and forty-five seconds of your $100 coming."

Any questions I had eluded me, and I stared vacantly up at him. "I'll start," he volunteered. "How do you get the best from people? How do you make them want to be victorious, to do a better job?" With the same breath he was about to spew out a third question, but his secretary buzzed him with a call. Pressing the speaker button on the phone, he asked, "Who is it?"

"Something about Don Quixote's horse," she said in a bewildered tone.

With that, Mr. Preisser swung his feet up on the desk, folded his arms across his chest and leaned back in his black leather chair.

"Vic, it's been burned!" the man on the other end of the phone wailed. "They've burned *Don Quixote's Horse!*"

"Dennis! It's good to hear from you, my friend!" Vic cajoled, not at all caught up in his friend's sense of tragedy. He then calmly asked, "*Who* did it?"

"Kids. Some kids in the Bay Area," the distraught man sobbed. "It's gone. Everything. Everything I've worked for. Do you realize the time I spent on him? Gone." Dennis Patton, the famed artist of *Don Quixote's Horse*—the sixty-foot-tall lathe and tin-lid masterpiece—literally wept. His magnificent sculpture had been touring the country, opening to rave reviews. Though Dennis had been a serious artist for nearly fifteen years, it was *Don Quixote's Horse* that finally earned him not only renown as a contemporary artist, but a much needed income as well. *Don Quixote's Horse* had graced the cover of nearly every important art and trade publication.

After long minutes of listening to Dennis's dire mourning, Vic interrupted. "Oh, Dennis, I am absolutely thrilled to hear this! I couldn't be happier for you! And, think of all the publicity you'll get—free, no less!"

A moment of stunned silence followed Vic's congratulatory remark.

"Happy for me?" Dennis questioned blankly. "It's easy for you to be sunny about this, it didn't happen to you!"

"That's right. It happened to *you*, you lucky duck. It's all in the way you look at it, my friend," Vic told him. "It's about perspective—just like the story of the two sons of an alcoholic. See, there were two brothers," Vic began. "One brother was an alcoholic, while the other hardly touched liquor at all. Someone asked the alcoholic, 'Why do you drink so much?' The man responded, 'That's easy. My father was an alcoholic. You might say I learned to drink at my father's knee.' The same person asked the brother who rarely drank, 'You don't drink. How come?' The man responded, 'That's easy. You see, my father was an alcoholic. You might say I learned not to drink at my father's knee.' Dennis, each man made a choice about the way in which he responded to the cards he was dealt."

"But, Vic," Dennis moaned, his words still dripping grief for the destroyed artwork that had taken nearly two years of his life to complete. "Finally, *finally,* I've created a piece that brought the kind of recognition and money I've dreamed of. Now it's gone. Gone. For you to say that nothing could be better for me is crazy. You're crazy!"

"Crazy all right! Crazy about your work," Vic roared. "*Don Quixote's Horse* was a masterpiece to be sure, but you've been dwelling on him too long. Now you can be fresh again. Nothing could be better than this for starting the creative juices flowing, for creating, for trying something new. What an opportunity you've been handed. You've got important work ahead of you, my friend! The world is waiting for your *next* masterpiece. Better start working on it!"

Breaking out in laughter, Dennis surrendered. "Why didn't I know I'd hear something like this from you?" His voice more confident and hopeful, he added, "You're right, of course."

After a brief exchange of things going on in their personal lives, the men said their good-byes.

While somewhat jarred by the words Vic Preisser shared with his friend, I was inspired by Vic's positive perspective.

"That was certainly an encouraging view you shared with your friend Dennis," I commented.

"Many years ago I learned a valuable lesson," Vic explained. "There was a certain U.S. Air Force colonel stationed in Europe, and the men who served under him consistently made it onto the air force's high-speed promotion list. This particular colonel was responsible for more field-grade and general officer appointments than any other individual in the air force. A group of us were selected to study him, to find out why he was so skilled at finding extraordinary people. For a month we sat in his office and studied his behavior, his interpersonal reactions with people, what he did and how he did it. What we learned was that his great gift was *making people feel important.*

"The colonel was *the* man to grant assignments in Europe. He had a red phone on his desk—a direct line to Washington. When an assignment came in from the Pentagon, the colonel would just look down the hall and call the first officer he saw into his office. The colonel would then say to the man, 'Your country needs you. The Pentagon thinks you are the best young officer in the air force, and they have instructed me to run interference for you and make sure no one gets in your way as you carry out this career-making assignment. Your orders are being cut. Go to it!' He would give them his card, and tell them to call any time they needed any help. You see, his reputation as an exemplary leader was well-founded. He made others feel important. He expected their best and got it. The colonel believed in *all* his men's abilities to triumph and excel, and so they did. I sincerely believe that anyone can do just about anything *if* he feels valued and important."

"And that's what you did for Dennis. You made him feel valued and important," I concluded.

Vic nodded. "Dennis is important," he stated. "Like all of us, he just needed to be reminded of it. His best work is yet to come. And it will come. Plus, he's got Chris Goodwin, an Iowa girl, in his life now. They're in love, and there's nothing like love to make you feel important, so we know we haven't seen the best of Dennis *yet!*"

"But you also gave him a whole new perspective on his calamity," I reminded him.

"Bettie," he said, "*success is not measured by your victories, but by how you recover from your failures*—and some sort of failures are inevitable. If we remind each other to persistently find creative solutions to life's little challenges, solutions that turn negatives into positives, then we'll urge each other on to greatness. Dennis just needed to be reminded of that today."

"Hmm," I murmured, wondering if perhaps that's why Dennis had turned to his friend after a loss of such magnitude. Vic offered a rainbow after the flood. The famed artist may very well have known that his friend Vic would help him recast this catastrophe in such a way that he could see the possibility of something good emerging from it— Dennis knew Vic would help him find a creative solution.

"Thank you for agreeing to the internship," I said. "I'm looking forward to it. I do have a question though. Why did you sign my university contract without knowing the terms of the agreement?"

"Two reasons," Vic said. "First, you were persistent in finding a creative solution to see me. I have those three secretaries out there for a reason. Anyone who gets past them has exercised the kind of creative problem solving that proves she's coming to see me on a matter of importance and is honestly able to measure up to the challenge of being a part of the solution and not just complaining about a problem. Second, you made me feel important. You offered me $100 for *five* minutes of my time!"

With these words, he handed me back my $100 bill.

Two hours after my five minutes were used up, I not only had my contract signed, but I had an offer for a six-month position as a paid consultant to head the state's team evaluating the educational needs of Iowa correctional institutions. Happily, I completed my internship and the consulting assignment.

The university had been right. Working with Mr. Preisser was an enormous learning experience in both form and substance. And yet, it was that call from Dennis Patton while I was in Vic Preisser's office that offered the best learning experience for me: When we encourage others toward triumph by believing in them and their importance, we inspire them to view catastrophe as an opportunity and to look for creative solutions. Vic Preisser believed in his friend's ability to triumph. Thus, Dennis was free to move beyond the paralysis caused by his despair over the destruction of *Don Quixote's Horse*. Vic's advice spurred Dennis onward so that he used his time and talents in a more productive way. Over the course of the next year, Dennis put his heart and soul into creating *Woman's Head*, a piece that, coincidentally, would become one of his many masterpieces.

By the time *Woman's Head* was completed, the burning of Dennis's statue—which tens of thousands of daily commuters saw and loved as they passed by it each day—had generated enough publicity and public sentiment to support rebuilding it completely in metal. Building the statue in metal was something that Dennis had yearned to do in the beginning, but he hadn't been able to afford it at that time. Now he was given carte blanche to recreate *Don Quixote's Horse* the way he had dreamed it could be.

After I'd written this story, I called Dennis to check the facts on his artworks. He and I talked about our mutual friends Vic and Joy, and about the enormous love Dennis shares with his wife, Chris, and their two little children. When we talked about the days of *Don Quixote's Horse*, Dennis told me a story I didn't know.

Seven years to the very day after *Don Quixote's Horse* was burned, a man called Dennis and asked if he might come visit the artist. Unbeknown to Dennis, the man was one of three men who, in their teens, set ablaze *Don Quixote's Horse.*

"I've come to plead for your forgiveness," the man said to Dennis. "I burned down *Don Quixote's Horse*, and I want you to know how sorry I am. And how that act changed my life. The morning after my two friends and I set it on fire, I was lying in bed. In another room, my dad was reading the *San Francisco Chronicle*. Suddenly he bellowed, 'Hey, some jerk burned down *Don Quixote's Horse*. It takes a really rotten kid to do that. If someone did something like that to me, I'd have him put away. And if it were my kid, I'd disown him.' Well, there I was lying in bed and I realized that *I* was that rotten kid. The night before I had been drinking and doing drugs, and I participated in a terrible thing, the burning of a statue that I really did think was quite wonderful. I felt really rotten. Well, I didn't do anything bad after that, even though I haven't done much good either. My two other friends are in prison now, not because of burning down *Don Quixote's Horse* but because they continued doing terrible things. So, maybe just the fact that I've stayed out of trouble is good, though I am a miserable man. But one thing is for sure, *Don Quixote's Horse* is responsible for my turnaround."

Even though the man had been punished by the state for the crime he committed in his youth, he asked how he could make personal restitution to Dennis. Dennis and the man talked about it, and they parted ways on good terms.

Some months later, the man's mother called Dennis. Crying, she said, "Thank you for giving me back my son. Whatever happened that day between the two of you, whatever you said, freed him. He's turned over a new leaf. He's working for the first time in years, and he's no longer a lost, bitter man. After a childhood of criminal behavior, after many hopeless, wasted years of adulthood, finally, finally, I have my son back."

"So, what did you tell him?" I asked Dennis.

Softly Dennis said, *"Success is not measured by your victories, but by how you recover from your failures!"* I could hear the emotion in his voice as he added, "It's really something isn't it? *Don Quixote's Horse* is the reason that young man turned his life around. Who could have known how important its destruction would turn out to be?"

As Vic expected, Dennis Patton has continued to create many new masterpieces. Among them are the Ph-Norks, larger-than-life birds in wild colors, all of them with stars in their eyes and with goofy grins. They're seen in stores all over the world. *Woman's Head* is a head, nearly one block long, of a woman, her face intricately carved of wood, her full head of dangling hair made up of the branches of trees. This stunning masterpiece has never sustained so much as a stolen twig from her head in the twenty years it has graced the land on which it sits. One of Dennis's more recent grandiose works can be seen at the Cedar Rapids, Iowa, airport. It is the figure of eight travelers, three times larger than life. They are holding hands and leaping through the air.

As for Vic, during my internship, I introduced him to my friend Joy at a social occasion sponsored by Vic's office. They fell in love and married two years later. As Vic said, "There's nothing quite like love to make you feel important."

4

Ageless Dance

"Bob! Bob T.!" the woman next to me instructed loudly, "Tell her why you wouldn't marry that one lady last year!"

Obediently, the man across the table, Bob T., gruffed, "Oh, her! That was the darndest thing! She told me if I wanted to marry her, I couldn't go to dances anymore! 'Well,' I said, 'I don't reckon I can do that.'" Looking at the woman who commanded that he tell the story, Bob T. reminded her, "June. June Stewart was her name. You remember Junie, don't you, Helen?"

"Course I do," Helen replied. "Wasn't anybody who could get all gussied up like June Stewart!" This she said good-naturedly. Looking in my direction, Helen informed me, "She said polishing belt buckles just wasn't her style."

His pearl-gray hairs carefully slicked back for his night out, Bob T. Barrett from Whitney, Texas, nodded in agreement. Looking ever so thoughtful, he earnestly admitted, "See, I'm lookin' to find me a woman to marry. But she's *gotta* like to dance." Bob T. paused while peering at me over the rim of his glasses, studying me carefully, perhaps wondering if he ought to be telling this to a perfect stranger. I must have met his litmus test. "My wife, Louise, died twelve years ago," he divulged. Then, as if revisiting a special memory, a long pause followed before he said softly, "I've been single ever since." He sighed deeply, then stated, "I thought I'd finally found someone, you know." Glancing in the direction of the floor, Bob T. shook his head from side to side and then completed his thought with, "But June there, she didn't dance and had no intentions of learnin'. That just won't work. Besides," he added indignantly, adjusting the sliding silver steer on his bolo tie, "she wanted me to take the jackass off the hood of my truck!"

"The *what?*" I asked, raising my eyebrows and venturing cautiously.

"The hood ornament on my truck!" Bob T. said, disgruntled all over again. "Why, my grandson, Kelly, helped me put that jackass on the hood." A wide grin washed across his face as he boasted, "Even wired it up so the eyes light up when I put on the brakes!" Then with all the resolution in the world, Bob T. Barrett declared, "And by gosh, on the hood it's gonna stay!" Turning to Helen he informed her, "Junie said she wouldn't ride in my truck until I took it off!

Can you imagine that?" Bob T. shook his head in disgust. Helen nodded in amused yet complete understanding.

In Dallas on business, I'd wandered into the dinner club nearest my hotel with hardly a glance at the sign announcing it was "Country Cross-Over Seniors Night." As he led me to a table, the waiter informed me, "There's still time for you to order, but the kitchen will be closing soon." I looked around. Crimson Crooners, a country band, was setting up. Nearly all the tables were full of seniors, obviously here for the dance. Feeling more than a little out of place—this was hardly the relaxing dinner after a long day's work that I'd envisioned—I contemplated leaving. But it was late, I was hungry and, since by this time I'd already been seated, I decided to stay.

My chance decision and subsequent encounter proved a delight. The crowd, while not raucous, was anything but lifeless. Like the mirrored globe hanging from the ceiling glittering its prisms of light across the dance floor, the room was filled with sparkling "old-timers" with bright smiles and dazzling Western wear—complete with hats, boots, buckles and bows. Animated chatter, spontaneous laughter, and the smells of Old Spice and cream perfume wafted through the air. As did many jokes, accompanied by the sounds of their listeners' laughter and gestures of slapping backs and knees in response to the joker's wit.

As the band struck up a lively two-stepper, the couples, holding hands, made their way to the dance floor, snapping their fingers, swaying, swooning and bobbing all the way to their spots. Some of the couples' synchronized styles were choreographed perfectly—perhaps as much from their years of dancing intimately with each other as from their mastery of the methodical and intricate steps required in country dancing. Other couples, their confident gaiety apparent, improvised to adapt to their partners' moves. Not at all inhibited—neither by personality nor by their arthritis, silver hair or deepening laugh lines—the seniors danced. Oh, how they danced!

And were transformed by it. There was something indescribably *alive* in their dancing, a radiance of sorts. I watched, mesmerized and enchanted by the animation: faces glowed, eyes sparkled, lips eagerly mouthed the words, limber shoulders swayed to the rhythm, quick feet moved to the beat of the music. All movements defied the dancers' ages. My eyes drifted to Bob—who moments ago complained about his arthritis—now swinging his latest partner this way and that; she thrilled in each maneuver.

The table next to mine grew so crowded that it overflowed, and I was soon included in the throng. Now returning from the dance floor, Helen looked at me and said breathlessly with a grin, "That's a great tune, isn't it? A real toe-tapper." When she reached for her chair at the friend-clustered table, all the men stood to help seat her.

"Sure is," I replied and then complimented, "You're really good out there. How long have you and your husband been dancing together?"

Pleased at the praise, she confided, "With this husband, just seventeen years. My first husband, Harold, passed away. He and I had well over thirty years of dancing together!" With a look of sassy satisfaction, she added, "When Clem asked me to marry him, I told him he had to promise me that we would go dancing once a week—no excuses!'" From his seat beside her, Clem chuckled and chimed in, "She sure did! But, hey, that was easy to promise. I mean, I get to hold my gal in my arms and dance, too. What could be better?" He wasn't looking for an answer, and no one offered one. However, Bob T. appeared riled (perhaps once again thinking of June Stewart and her nerve in suggesting otherwise) and proclaimed, "I go to *every* dance I can. This place has one every Wednesday and there's one every other Saturday at the Hilton, but the best ones are at the Senior Center at the Elks Lodge on Fridays."

Looking around the room at these happy and exuberant seniors, I wondered if it was dancing that caused them to "gussy up" and brought them out in such great numbers. Or was it the socialization, the fun and connection of being in each other's company? I decided to ask.

"What's so special about dancing, Bob?" I asked.

"Great exercise. Great fun," came his reply, as though it needed no explaining.

"So is swimming, even walking," I responded, hoping to engage him in conversation.

He was uncompromising. "No, no!" Bob T. said defiantly, waving toward the dance floor. "*Nothing* compares to dancing! If it weren't for dancing, we'd all be sitting home on the couch watching TV." Wryly he declared, "That's no way to live!" He pondered for a moment and then added what I think was perhaps one of the most important reasons so many came that night: "Dancing keeps me young. Don't feel any of my aches and pains when I'm dancin'!" With a whimsical expression, Bob T. professed, "Out there, I'm *young* again. Just feel more alive. I'm *ageless* when I'm dancin'!" Sounds and nods of agreement circled the table.

The band started to play a twangy tune. Immediately Bob T. stood up and announced, "Time to polish the belt buckle, boys!" Scouting the room for a partner, his eyes scanned the crowd—but stopped when he noticed a petite woman smartly dressed in black slacks and a white blouse heavily studded with multicolored rhinestones. She stood near the entrance of the room. At first he looked startled, but that look was quickly replaced by a coy smile. In a hushed tone that held both surprise and delight, he declared, "Well, I'll be!"

Bob T. Barrett wasted no time getting over to June Stewart. Hitching up his pants, Bob T. checked his fly, straightened his bolo tie and sauntered across the room in the direction of the pretty redheaded woman who now stood with a bevy of would-be dance partners around her.

"Look at June!" Helen exclaimed to no one in particular. All of us already were.

Then softly—almost under her breath—Helen revealed, "She *finally* came in."

Clem was busy with his own observation. "Just look at how nervous ol' Bob is," he chuckled with obvious amusement. "I think he was missing June more than he let on."

The once-gruff seventy-six-year-old "Texas boy" now stood meekly in front of June, his head lowered, his cowboy hat off, held with both hands. They stood together talking—until June gestured toward the dance floor. With a big grin on his face, Bob T. escorted his Junie to the dance floor, draped an arm around her, and slowly and delicately directed her moves to the romantic ballad now being played.

He needn't have been so cautious and deliberate. When the next tune picked up the pace June quickly adapted and moved into an appropriate set of moves for the beat and tempo. It was in perfect step that June Stewart and Bob T. danced. Oh, how they danced.

"Ol' Bob can really polish the belt buckle, can't he!" Clem exclaimed while watching Bob and June. "And just look at the two of them together. She's really got the steps down!"

"Polish the belt buckle?" I mimicked, having never heard the term before that night. "I've heard that phrase several times this evening. *Exactly* what does it mean?"

"Means holding someone up close, you know," Helen explained with a sly grin, moving her eyebrows up and down and motioning toward the dance floor where Bob and June were executing yet a new routine of steps in perfect harmony.

When the tune ended, Bob approached the band, no doubt making a request for a special song. Within moments, a slow, sweet, country waltz-like melody began. As though it was "their song," a beaming Bob reached out to his Junie, and the two folded into each other's arms. She leaned her head upon his chest, closed her eyes. Smiling, they swayed together—presumably "polishing belt buckles."

"Look at that girl!" exclaimed Helen with a look of genuine satisfaction on her face. "She's hopelessly in love with her Bob T."

"'Girl'?" I remarked. "It's interesting to hear you say

that. I call my best girlfriends 'girl.' It's a term of endear-
ment. Even so, I never considered that I might call them
'girls' when they are in their sixties and seventies. But I
hope I do. It sounds so delightful."

"Oh, we always call each other 'girls' when we're having
fun," Helen replied. "Come to think of it, mostly it's when
we're at dances. When we're here, we're so full of life, full
of gaiety. We laugh and giggle and flirt. You know, like
girls."

"Yes, I do," I said. "I know I love the *girl* in me and hope
to preserve as much of *her* for as long I can—like you *girls*
here tonight!"

Observing Bob and June dancing, Helen commented
thoughtfully, "Bob, more than anyone else, brings out the
girl in June."

"She does look happy," I commented and then asked,
"You made a comment earlier about June 'finally' coming
in. What did you mean?"

"Oh, gosh," replied Helen. "I thought I'd never get those
two together! 'You're going to have to learn to dance if you
want old Bob T. Barrett,' I told June. 'Let him teach you
how to dance so you can enjoy it together.'

"'Oh, no,' June told me. 'I can't do that. I'd be too
embarrassed.'

"'Well, then,' I told her. 'Take private lessons.' She did."

"Didn't Bob know?" I asked.

"No, no one did," Helen replied. "She especially didn't
want Bob to know, so I wasn't about to tell him. And he
didn't know she planned to come here tonight. She came
with me. But when we arrived, she got cold feet about

coming in so she told me to go ahead in and that she'd be along when she was ready." Breaking out in delighted laughter, Helen added, "Poor thing. She's been sitting out there in the car for an hour!" Looking in the direction of the dance floor where her friends, Bob T. and June, danced in each other's arms, Helen's voice softened. "But just look at them now!"

When the band took a break, Bob T. approached, grinning sheepishly and holding hands with June. Introducing her he asked, "You all know Junie, don't you?" But before anyone could answer, Bob looked at Clem and inquired, "How much that ol' Lincoln run you?"

"What do you mean?" Clem asked.

"Well, I just might want me one," Bob retorted.

"Why would you want one of those when you've got that fancy truck?" Clem questioned.

"Well, my wife-to-be," Bob T. said, looking mooningly at June, "just might like one of those big ol' four-doors."

5

The Jeweler's Touch

"Oh, Mom, it's even my birthstone! Isn't it just beautiful?" My daughter had swooned when she spotted the ring in the jeweler's window. Standing side by side, we had delayed our journey to the restaurant down the street to admire the sparkles of its unique setting and artistically off-center stones. Her blue-green eyes danced with delight. She was clearly enchanted with the ring. Smiling, she said coyly, "Buying it for me sure would be a nice touch, Mom!"

Since her fairly recent move out of state, I missed her so much. Though we spoke on the phone regularly, I longed for her presence. Thoughts of her tugging at my heart, I decided to send a gift as a token of my love. Bandying about ideas of just what the right gift might be, I recalled her delight as she gazed at the ring. It seemed the perfect gift. After all, rings are a symbol of union and connection. A ring for her would be, in her own words, a "nice touch."

I stood at the jewelry counter carefully scrutinizing the glittering stones and creative settings in the brilliantly polished glass case. When I pointed to the setting my daughter had admired, the dark-haired, dark-eyed jeweler smiled demurely, opened the case and retrieved the ring. He held the beautiful gleaming ring up in the air, eyeing it from a distance. Then he examined the stone closely with his loupe. Next, strangely enough, he blew a little puff of air on it, as though it were dusty. His final act of preparing the piece of jewelry for my inspection was to meticulously shine it with the chamois cloth he carried in his back pocket. Finally pleased with the ring, he smiled, handed it to me and explained, "The scintillation of this ring is superb!"

As I examined the *scintillation* of the ring, a young girl— perhaps seven or eight years of age—walked in. Steps behind the girl, a woman followed. I presumed she was the girl's mother. Upon seeing them, the jeweler's serene demeanor changed instantly. His solemn yet friendly face lit up with a beaming smile. His dark tranquil eyes suddenly transformed, radiating joy, shining with an extraordinary sparkle far surpassing any of the stones in the case.

With a customer to his right and the mother with daughter to his left, the professional jeweler had no trouble deciding who should wait for his attention. "Please," he begged humbly. "You must *please* excuse me for a moment."

Raising his hand, he motioned me to wait and reiterated courteously, "*Please* excuse me."

By now, the little girl, her dark shoulder-length hair held back from her face with a brown barrette, stood in front of him. With eyes glimmering like a Fourth of July sparkler, the jeweler looked lovingly into the little girl's dark eyes—ones the exact shade of brown as his own. Placing his right hand knowingly on her shoulder, the jeweler then reached out to touch her small face with his left hand, his eyes never leaving hers as he smiled sincerely and deeply into them. He continued to look at her, his smile lingering.

As if there was yet more love of which he was capable, without letting go of the small girl's face he then turned to the woman next to her, obviously his wife. Gently lifting his right hand from the small girl's shoulder, the jeweler reached out his hand and held the woman's arm, now shifting his loving gaze to her eyes. Though he spoke no words, he might as well have shouted out loud, "Thank you for this child," or maybe something even more seductive, for these moments revealed an absolute and reverent love story.

It was a stunningly precious moment, one in which this family escaped to a world of their own. Such a tender enchantment of love.

Oh, to love—and be loved—in such a way!

After viewing and comparing several rings, I decided to buy my daughter the exquisite little stone in the setting she so desired, the one she thought would be a "nice touch." But it was the jeweler's touch that made *sending* it to her incomplete. So I made arrangements to fly out to visit her because I wanted to give her *more* than the connection of a symbolic gift of love. I wanted to give her a gift as profound as the one the jeweler had given his family that day—the gift of his loving gaze and touch.

To *honor* love is a simple yet profound gift—and a taste berry available to us all.

6 His Brother's Keeper

It was a perfectly beautiful fall weekend, ideal for being outdoors. White cumulus clouds, with thin feathers of the cirrus high above them, drifted against the brilliant blue September sky. The sun's rays sufficiently warmed the skin, yet it was pleasantly cool. And though a crisp stillness hung in the air, the surrounding treetops stirred. All calendars aside, Mother Nature hadn't yet made up her mind if she should allow fall to linger or plunge into winter.

Best friends Ben and Robert were less ambiguous. The perfect weather was definitely the deciding factor in planning a weekend hike up into the high mountains, a trip they had made many times together over the years. De-stressing, male bonding, regrouping: That was how they described their simple love and respect for the outdoors and for this beautiful mountainous region they loved to explore.

This excursion, like many others they had on the north face of this same mountain, was a three-day, two-night expedition. Even the "game plan" remained the same: The first day's exuberant eight-mile hike up the north side of the mountain would place them about three-fourths of the way to the top. Here they would set up base camp beside the familiar massive, ancient granite rock, a formation that served as a lookout point and doubled as marker and windbreak for a campsite. On the second day they would continue making their way to the top; their goal was to reach it by noon. After lunching and resting there, the men would begin a leisurely descent, intent on reaching their base camp at dusk. After camping there for the night, on the third and final day they would complete their journey to the bottom of the mountain.

They began their trip on Friday morning, early.

"I'm really going to enjoy this," Ben said, as they began their hike up the mountain.

"Yup," Robert confirmed. "We need to do this more often. I know I need to. Though with the baby due in just five weeks, this will probably be my last trip of this season."

"Well, we couldn't have chosen a better weekend!" said his friend.

The men arrived at the first destination on schedule. They set up camp and prepared for the next two days before retiring for the evening.

Early the next morning, they climbed up on the huge granite rock to survey the spectacular mountain range and valley. Just like the day before, the overhead skies were the bluest of blues, and there was a slight northerly breeze. The two friends began their day's journey.

The next few hours were enjoyable and seemed to pass quickly for the men. At times, both walked in complete silence, staring intently at the ground before them, seemingly consumed by their own thoughts. Sometimes this reverie produced an isolated comment on one aspect or another of either's job or a business associate; at other times, an opinion was rendered on a score, or an athlete, or a favorite sports team. On several different occasions, the men engaged in a lively conversation about one of their children. Mostly, however, their spoken words were employed to compare and discuss rare vegetation or for alerting the other to an element of nature around them such as a wildflower in bloom, or the doe discovered feeding on mountain grass nearby. "Look, over there," Robert whispered to his companion, pointing in the direction of the deer. "Beautiful, isn't she! Hand me the camera, but be as quiet as you can so we don't scare her away." Silently, they crept closer. When the click of the camera frightened her and she darted away, their voices uttered no words, merely sounds: "Ohhh! Mmmh."

When Mother Nature had sufficiently seduced the men with her creativity and beauty, they became spirited boys, offering up their lighthearted playfulness. "You're standing in poison ivy!" Rob shouted, pointing in the direction of Ben's feet. "Just kidding!" he laughed, when Ben leaped away from where he stood. Next came an animated discussion of past antics and then jokes. "Hey, Rob," Ben began, "Did you hear the one about the hiker who got poison ivy on his . . . ?" A long string of jokes followed, each man coming to a full halt as respect was paid to the other's witticism. Time stood still—as did the men—while each carefully scrutinized the eyes, mouth and hand gestures of the jokester. No facial expression or pause pertinent to the punchline was lost. Like the previous trips, this outing in the midst of the beauty of nature was fulfilling the goal of a reprieve—brief though it was—from the obligations and responsibilities that now seemed to characterize the nature of their lives.

The men arrived at the summit nearly two hours later than planned. As they sat on the top of the mountain and ate, they became more aware of their surroundings and were surprised that the wind was picking up and the temperature dropping. Both men silently observed the dark cloud front slowly moving in their direction.

"I say we start back now and forgo the siesta, Rob. What do you think?" Ben asked. Rob agreed. The men put on their backpacks and began their exodus down the mountain.

Within the hour, electrical flashes lit up the distant sky and a low rumbling of far-off thunder could be heard. The men realized a major storm front was moving in. "This could hit by morning," Ben warned. "I'm cold. I think I'll put on my coat. Want yours?"

"Yes," Rob said, taking his parka. "It looks a little *too* stormy to suit me. I think we better pick up our pace and get back down to the campsite as quickly as we can."

An hour later, the weather conditions intensified. Dust and twigs whisked in relentless gusts all around them. Clutching their jackets—now zipped all the way to their chins—the men fought against the force of the ever-brazen wind as they made their way down the trail. Ben didn't bother hiding his anxiety. "Listen to that wind howl," he yelled so that his friend could hear him. "I don't like the sound of this."

Not only did the wind howl, within a half hour snow started falling. Over the next hour, Old Man Winter delivered an inch of snow. In the next two hours, he dropped an ankle-deep blanket. The unrelenting wind—now gusting at nearly forty miles an hour—slapped them with icy cold snowflakes, stinging their skin like a swarm of attacking bees. With their collars pulled up and the bills of their caps pulled down over their eyes for protection, they trudged along, with each step crunching into a cushion of newly fallen snow.

By midday, the trail was indiscernible. The snow now crept over the tops of their hiking boots.

Needing a reprieve from the cold driving wind and blizzardy snow, the men found themselves stopping frequently to huddle in the protective shelter of a tree or clump of bushes. The hike to the camp that should have taken them five hours was looking more like seven to eight.

With each man concentrating to ward off the invading, aching cold and buck the fierce wind, it was nearly impossible to talk to each other, so they exchanged few words. Instead, each man periodically reached out to the other, vigorously rubbing his companion's shoulders, to help the circulation, produce warmth and relieve the weight of the packs.

The weather conditions showed no signs of letting up. Since both men knew the severity of these types of storms, they knew they couldn't afford to be stranded. They could be snowed in for days—even weeks. "This doesn't look good," Ben yelled over the wind's howl.

"We'll be cutting it real close," Robert yelled back, his tone grave. "This storm could drop six to eight feet, and with *this* wind, drifts of ten to fifteen feet!"

"We'll never make it out if we stay overnight when we reach camp like we planned," Ben warned.

"On the other hand, I'm exhausted, and we're not dressed for this. Maybe we should reach base camp, wait this out for a few hours, and see if there's some letup," Rob proposed. "We're right smack in the heart of this storm; maybe it'll break by morning."

"No. We can't chance it," Ben retorted. "We'll freeze to death by morning if we don't get out of here. We need to put what food we have left in our pockets, drop our packs here, head for the shelter, stop just long enough to build a fire to warm up, put a reserve of food in our pockets, get our gloves and warmer night gear, and leave for home." Aware that Rob still questioned the wisdom of not staying in their tent's tenuous shelter for the night to see if the storm would let up, he reasoned further, "We're talking about covering a distance that takes a full day in favorable conditions, Rob. Every minute is crucial." Knowing his friend was right, Rob nodded in approval.

The weather continued to worsen and now, grueling

minutes felt like torturous hours. Each step was an exhausting, painful exertion in snow that buried each man over his knees. With the weather growing worse and miles still left to go, both wondered how long it would take them to even reach the shelter. Home now seemed like an eternity away. United in their goal and working together as a team, the friends took turns in the lead breaking the trail. When one man was no longer able to exert the energy it took to continue to plow through the deepening snow drifts, the other took over.

Rob seemed the most tired. Seeing his partner's shoulders heave as he tried to catch his breath, Ben yelled, "Are you doing okay up there?" Even though Robert hadn't been in the lead for long, Ben knew his friend wasn't as fit and strong as he was. "Let's switch again," he offered. "You've been up there for a while." As he moved past him to switch places, he patted Rob's back in encouragement.

"I don't know how much longer I can keep this up," Rob panted.

"We'll keep it up as long as we have to," Ben said with conviction. "We've got a lot of people counting on us at home." Two weary and determined men continued to trudge through the storm-shrouded daylight hours.

It was nearly six o'clock by the time they reached camp. Scooping the snow drifts off their small tent—which had collapsed under the gusts of wind and snow and blown up against the granite rock—they squeezed inside the drooping shelter. "You sure we shouldn't try to wait it out up here?" Rob asked. His question was nearly rhetorical; he, too, knew that it would be impossibly dangerous to stay.

Not only had the storm shown no signs of letting up, it had worsened.

"No," Ben stated emphatically. "We can't even get a fire started. We've got to high-tail it out of these mountains as fast as we can." Robert nodded in agreement, and both rummaged through their gear to find the few articles of warmer clothing they had brought for the colder mountain nights—never expecting that cold would plummet to the depths they now confronted.

"How long do you think it will take us?" Rob asked, gratefully yanking on his gloves.

"It's hard to tell," Ben admitted. "But if we just keep moving, we should do okay. Here's the plan then: We follow the trail, and if we lose it, we follow the landmarks. We know this area like the back of our hands. We should do okay. We just keep moving."

"Okay," came the response from his longtime friend.

For the next two strenuous and grueling hours, the men pretty much repeated their behavior prior to reaching base camp, the difference being that both had tired, night was falling and the visibility had shortened to about two feet. "Hey, Ben, what's that?" Robert asked, pointing at what appeared to be a rock formation. "I know we aren't off course . . . are we?"

"No, I recognize that pine next to that slope," Ben called back against the howling wind. "We're still on the trail. Let's check it out." The men kneeled down, patted the dark formation and brushed away several inches of snow. To their dismay—and horror—it was the body of a man.

Leaning over the man, Ben placed his face next to his.

"He's still breathing," Ben panted. And then, speaking loudly so that the stranger might hear him, Ben questioned, "Can you hear me? You gotta get up! We'll help you. Can you stand up? Come on. Get up!" Ben vigorously rubbed the man's shoulders and gently shook him, but the collapsed form didn't stir.

Rob tried. Dropping to his knees, he rubbed the freezing man's hands and chest, shouting, "Hey! Come on! You have to wake up!"

"How long has he been here?" Ben questioned, adding, "It couldn't be very long, or else he'd be frozen to death. We've got to get him to safety."

With these words came the sudden realization that Rob and Ben were faced with a new problem: Here was a person, alive and needing immediate help. It was a dilemma they hadn't thought would be a part of their plight. Unexpectedly caught in the hostile, bitter and deadly freezing cold of a winter storm, one that reached the perilous stage of a whiteout—the most serious and life-threatening of storm conditions—Ben and Rob had all they could do to struggle for their own survival. The two men looked at each other and then down at the unconscious man. Both knew that their lives were on the line—as was the life of the freezing man in the snow.

"We don't have a choice," Rob reasoned, "There's no way we can help him."

"We can't just leave him here. He'll die," Ben retorted.

"Listen, Ben," Rob said, "our only chance—and *his* only chance—is to keep going and send back help!" Seeing Ben shake his head, refusing to comply with his way of thinking,

Rob continued, "Remember what you said—we've got a lot of people counting on us. Think of Beth and the kids!"

"I can't leave him, Rob. I just can't. He'll die before help arrives."

His frustration mounting, Rob pleaded, "You said it yourself: We have to do whatever it takes. Besides, how can we get him down? He can't walk. He's dead weight, we can't carry him. Come on, Ben, we'll send help back for him."

Ben shook his head again. "No, Rob," he said, meeting his eyes. "I won't leave him."

"Damn it, Ben!" Rob yelled. "I'm going! With you or without you—I'm going!" Ben said nothing. Their eyes met and held a second, then darted apart. His movements stiff, Rob turned hesitantly and once again started down the trail, leaving the stranger and Ben—his friend of nearly twenty years—behind. He walked a short distance, then stopped and turned around, hoping that his friend might be following. He was not. So urged on by his will to survive, to get back to his family and, now, to send back help for the other two men, Rob turned and headed toward home.

Mustering all his strength, Ben hoisted the unconscious man onto his back, draping the man's arms over his own shoulders. Even though Ben was a big man, and the older man was smaller and lighter, he had his work cut out for him. Holding the man's arms in front of his neck, Ben leaned over and began slowly making his way down the trail, with the man's feet dragging through the snow behind them. Soon, he was surrounded in darkness, so he concentrated solely on taking step after step, one foot in front of the other. The trees, standing as sentinels on each side of the trail, guided the way. "We'll make it," he grunted aloud from time to time, as if offering the oblivious man comfort and assurance. Then, he reassured himself. "I can do this!" he said, his tone determined. "I can do this!"

As time passed and fatigue set in, the weight of the man became unbearable. Ben knew he must coax and encourage himself or else it would be nearly impossible for him to continue. He willed himself to think of positive thoughts, happy moments and joyful events. Perhaps singing would distract him and keep his spirits high. He began a cadence, mentally counting off the distance to safety: "Ninety-nine bottles of beer on the wall, ninety-nine bottles of beer, take one down, pass it around, ninety-eight bottles of beer on the wall. Ninety-eight bottles of beer . . ." The memory of the first time he sang this song—from beginning to end— with a group of college buddies caused him to chuckle, and he grinned. Yes, he'd sing *this* song; it would see him down the mountain.

The sheer task of lugging the man on his back increased his body temperature, and soon the man on his back felt more like a protective pelt warming his back than a slab of ice, as he had at first. With this new sensation, Ben started thinking about the man he carried. *Who is he? Does he have a family at home worrying about where he is right now? Is he married? Does he have children? Or grandchildren?* He tried to imagine the man was someone he deeply loved—his wife . . . his son . . . his father . . . his brother . . . his friend Rob.

Plowing through the snow, leaning forward in almost a controlled downhill fall, Ben refused to surrender to the urge to stop and catch his breath. He so badly wanted—

needed—a rest, but he knew if he stopped he wouldn't have the strength to get the man back up on his back and start again. "Nineteen bottles of beer on the wall, nineteen bottles of beer, take one down, pass it around, eighteen bottles of beer on the wall. . . ." Ben took both of the man's hands in one of his own and fumbled at a packet of food in his pocket. It seemed impossible to get out, so he gave up on the idea. His exhaustion squeezing his lungs and weighting his body, he felt a stark terror as he began to doubt his own ability to go on. "You're going to make it, aren't you, Ben?" he asked himself aloud. This was followed by, "Maybe you won't," and then "What would it be like to die out here? Would I just lie down and fall asleep and never wake up again?" Ben even wondered what thoughts had gone through this man's head when he collapsed from the cold. "Sixteen bottles of beer on the wall, sixteen . . ."

Ben thought about how painful it would be to never see Beth and his children again, or not to be with her on their children's birthdays, or not see their graduations, weddings . . . or grandchildren. "We always teased each other about growing old and gray together," he said out loud, and with that thought savored the memory of Beth's hair. It was long, soft and shiny; he liked to feather it between his fingers. A small smile pulled at his lips. As if a new wave of reassurance set in, he said, "I *can't* die out here. I *won't* die out here." These words renewed his energy and so he continued, putting one foot in front of the other, taking the next step. And the next. . . .

He tried to remember every detail of the birth of each

of his children and the incredible sensations of joy and overwhelming love he experienced with each birth. He smiled at the idea that within the next two months Rob and his wife would welcome their second child into the world. He wondered if by now Rob was home and had sent help on the way to get him and the man he carried.

His thoughts turned once again to his wife. He smiled at the thought of the risqué love note she had slipped into his packed gear, knowing he would find it as he unpacked that first night at the campsite. He revisited the memories of the day he met Beth, and marveled at how compatible they were and how good they were for each other. He traced with his mind every curve, line and angle of her form. "Thirty-one bottles of beer on the wall, thirty-one bottles of . . ."

He paused, muddled as to whether this was his fifth or sixth time through the song, only to start over again.

As the dim light of a new day illuminated the horizon, he passed the familiar trail mark telling him that help and shelter couldn't be that much farther away. It wasn't.

In the distance, he spotted the snow-hazed flashing red lights. And in that instant, everything changed. Now ecstatic and half-delirious, he shouted and cried at the same time: "Oh, thank God! We're going to make it! We're going to live!" Quickly, he leaned down so that the man on his back would slide off, handling him carefully and gently laying him down. And then, his arms flailing in the air, he shouted at the top of his lungs, "Hey! Up here! We're up here!" He hoped that his voice could be heard over the blowing wind, so he repeated his pleas. "Up here! We're up here! Help! We need help!" Exhilarated by the nearness of assistance, and spurred on by renewed energy, Ben tried to run, but stumbled instead. He got up, stumbled again, and once again got up, all the while shouting, "Help! We need help! Over here!"

Closer now, he could make out that the flashing lights were from police vans and an ambulance. Knowing for sure that help had arrived freed up any control he had been keeping on his emotions. With his gratitude and elation came a stream of tears: He was *alive*; help had arrived. He would be reunited with hisfamily, friends, and Rob, and the man he had carried was now in the hands of help.

When two men from the rescue team rushed to his side, Ben allowed himself to feel the full extent of his pain and exhaustion. He collapsed in their arms.

Now between two rescue workers, his arms hanging over their shoulders, Ben leaned on them in order to walk at all. "You've got to get him help, fast," Ben huffed, flinging an arm in the direction of where the older man lay a short distance behind him. "He's in bad shape." When Ben looked over his shoulder, he saw that men from the rescue team were already attending to him.

As they drew closer to the base of the mountain, Ben saw other rescue workers huddled over something on the trail. As he and the two men supporting him came upon the small gathering, Ben recognized the familiar hat and coat.

It was Rob.

Frantic at this realization, Ben bellowed, "Is he okay? Is he going to be all right?" When the man on each side of him looked to each other in silence, Ben knew the answer to his question.

"I'm sorry," replied the rescue worker to his left. "Nothing could have protected him from this kind of cold, he didn't have adequate clothing. . . ." Looking at Ben and seeing he was also dressed in only jeans and a parka, he said, "You're lucky to be alive." Pointing to the man Ben had carried on his back, he added, "The additional warmth generated by carrying that man's body saved your life—and his."

Two men—each faced with a decision. Each made a choice; neither choice wrong, just different. In the end, it was Ben's style of brotherhood that saved not only a stranger's life, but also his own.

7

Everyone Can't Be President

Skipping home from the corner where the school bus dropped her off, Jenaye, a little neighbor, spotted me getting my mail. "Guess what?" she gleefully called out to me, "My class is putting on a play next week at school! In it there'll be a beautiful fairy princess with long shiny hair, and she gets to wear beautiful fairy wings and a long pink dress and carry a glittering gold wand!" Prancing around, the darling seven-year-old's angelic face was animated with her joy. Breathlessly she announced, "I'm trying out for the part!" Clapping her hands, she giggled with glee. Sparing no excitement she announced, "It's a musical and we get to sing!"

"Wow! The fairy princess!" I exclaimed, properly impressed.

Jenaye nodded with fervent enthusiasm. "A fairy princess who wears glitter on her shoes and glitter in her hair, and a sparkling gold crown—my teacher said it's a 'tee-air-a'—on her head!" Jenaye twirled around and modeled the imaginary dress. Her hands glided over that flowing gown, smoothed the unseen wings sprouting from her shoulders and adjusted the invisible tiara. Then, she turned and skipped toward home, merrily singing off-key as she went.

The following week, while once again at my mailbox, I noticed Jenaye's mother, Jade, waiting for her daughter at the school bus stop. Within moments, the bus stopped and Jenaye, ever effervescent, hopped down its steps and ran to her mother, laughing and chattering nonstop as she went. Hand in hand, mother and daughter walked toward their home. Upon seeing me, Jenaye pulled away and came skipping over. "Guess what!" she enthused, "The tryouts for the *singing play* were today!" She was so overjoyed, I naturally assumed she'd landed her coveted role.

"Oh, you got the part of the fairy princess!" I cheered.

Jenaye shook her long brown curls and corrected, "No, I got the part of a flower! They selected *me* to be the flower!"

"A flower?" I asked, trying to conceal my amusement.

"Yes!" she explained with glee. "And I get to wear flower purple petals and green tights and leotards." Jenaye modeled imaginary petals springing from her hair with the same delight as she had modeled the fairy princess's "tee-air-a."

"That's wonderful!" I congratulated her. Knowing how much she had looked forward to singing, I asked, "What song will the flower sing?"

"Oh," she replied with wide-eyed innocence, "the flower part doesn't get to sing out loud, but it does get to whisper the words, but *silently*." She gently touched a tiny finger to her lips.

As she skipped up the driveway, her mother looked from me to Jenaye, then shook her head and smiled wryly. "She never ceases to amaze me. Nearly every child has a speaking or singing part, and Jenaye gets *selected* to be a silent flower, and *still* she's happy."

"Oh, for seeing the world through the eyes of a child!" I remarked wistfully. "Such open-ended acceptance."

"Yes, it's delightful," Jade agreed, with obvious appreciation for the gift of parenting this vivacious—and appreciative—little girl. "Jenaye has a real knack for seeing the cup as half full as opposed to half empty. Whenever I feel discouraged, I need only spend time with that joyful little spirit to be reminded of how beneficial it is to see life through the optimistic eyes of *possibility*."

"What is the source of her joy?" I asked. "I've watched her over these past years and she's continually upbeat, as though she always 'wins.' Any outcome is seen as a victory. Do you think Jenaye is simply immersed in the magical times of youthful faith and optimism, or is her unconquerable spirit a function of her personality? Or, is it because of your parenting? You're such a devoted mother."

"It's who she is," Jade replied, "though I'll never forget the experience that taught me the importance of helping

Jenaye look at life through the lens of seeing the positive. The night you took me to that reception at the chamber of commerce meeting was insightful."

It was over four years ago, shortly after I first met Jade and her family when they moved into my neighborhood. As a gesture of friendship and a way to get to know her, I took Jade to the social reception at a chamber of commerce meeting I was attending. At the chamber's reception, we stood in groups of seven to eight people, each of us introducing ourselves to the others and sharing information about the nature of our work and position.

"I'm the president of First Century Bank," said a distinguished-looking gentleman in the group.

"Oh, wonderful," said the others, obviously impressed.

"I'm the president of Edge Computers," said a smartly dressed young man. Once again the group members expressed their approval.

"I'm president of Globe Cell Phones, a company new to Southern California," said the young woman next in the circle of chamber members and their guests. Now distributing her business card to each of us she added, "Before the year end, I'm sure each of you will become a happy client!" Everyone in the group smiled, acknowledging her enthusiastic salesmanship.

When all eyes turned to me, I said, "I'm a professor of graduate studies at the university and the president of Instruction and Professional Development, a nationwide consulting firm."

"Oh, how interesting," said the others, again impressed.

Jade, smartly dressed for the occasion in a bright red silk suit, was the last of the group to share. Turning to her, the group nodded that it was her turn.

"I'm home full-time caring for my young daughter," she informed them.

Before Jade could say another word, the president of the computer company remarked, "Oh, just a homemaker." He tactfully turned his shoulder away from Jade, standing to his immediate right, and struck up a conversation with the bank president standing to his left. He was clearly uninterested in hearing anything further from Jade.

Introductions now over, one by one each member selected someone he or she deemed interesting or worthy of further comments and questions. The once large circle was now broken down into three small groups. Everyone was busy chatting with someone—with the exception of Jade.

"You see," Jade admitted, recalling that day, "the members of the group obviously assigned more importance to being a president than to being, in one man's words, 'just a homemaker.' They weren't all that interested in what someone at home caring for a small child might have to offer.

"But the experience was a good one in that the blatant rejection stung and made me wonder momentarily if I'd made the right decision when just the year before I had given up my lucrative, prestigious position for being at home full-time. Yet I knew that I made the right choice, *and* that I didn't like the way I was feeling now. At that moment I felt like what I was doing wasn't as important as being president, and I knew that not to be true. I realized how important it was to help Jenaye develop an outlook that made her realize that what she did was important regardless of the value others placed on it.

There are times in life when she will get selected to be the fairy princess, and there are times, like today, when she won't. I want her to be happy, either way. And most especially, I want her to find joy in the parts for which she is selected. While I do want Jenaye to desire to be president, I don't want her to use it as the measuring stick for whether or not she's happy."

I looked to Jenaye, now using the sidewalk as an imaginary hopscotch board. "I don't think you have to worry, Jade," I commented. "Jenaye is a healthy little girl with a very happy spirit—one who obviously feels very happy in being selected as president of silent flowers today!"

"Yes," her mother agreed. "Finding joy and possibility in playing the role of the silent flower rather than disappointment in not playing a glittering singing princess can be very magical!"

And a very useful taste berry!

8 The Ritual

They walked out of the dusty horizon, feet clopping in flopping sandals, arms draped across each other's shoulders, their animated faces aglow with lively chatter. In varying shades of olive skin, at varying heights of "small" and with varying lengths of long black hair—the youngest's a mass of curls—all three little girls were stunning in their innocent beauty. Though disheveled and dressed in tattered clothes, the appeal of their tiny frames, joyous demeanor and close-knit union was a tender—if not delightful—sight. Properly taking their place at the back of the line at the center that provided destitute families with a daily meal, they courteously and patiently waited, clasping each other's hands, each pair of their large eyes, like polished ebony orbs framed by thick long lashes, keeping a steady vigil over each other.

"When did you eat?" the nine-year-old asked.

"Yesterday, here," came one reply. The third little girl, saying nothing, nodded in assent. A stomach rumbled among them and three friends giggled in unison.

Each now carrying a tortilla and a bowl filled with rice and beans (the standard appropriation from the center), the girls scurried to the nearby shade of the glorious, bowed old banyan—one they fondly referred to as their "bent" tree. Reaching the familiar, well-worn patch of earth beneath its branches, they kicked off their sandals and squatted down, modestly tucking their ample colorful skirts around their slender brown legs.

From the far end of the other side of the tree, an old woman, her gray hair braided and wound tightly around her head, glanced up from her work and flickered a friendly gap-toothed smile their way. "Buenos días, mi hijitas," she greeted absently.

"Buenos días, Nana Chela," they chorused respectfully, although they were quite certain the old woman was deaf —and perhaps feeble. At the unrehearsed harmony of their greeting, the little girls looked at each other, unable to control a ripple of giggles.

No one at the center seemed to know much about the old woman, not from whence she came, nor of her family, not even if she worked for the need of money or the need of something to do. She didn't partake in meals served at the center, nor did she look hungry or destitute. Yet each day she appeared, toiling diligently, shaping and tying together tufts of straw to make dolls. First forming a round knot for a head between a tuft of straw atop and a longer one below, she fashioned a straw ponytail at her creation's nape, tying a bright ribbon around it. Next, fingers flying, she braided arms on either side of the torso below, then tied a bright apronlike skirt around its waist. Finally, with a paintbrush from the basket kept at her side, she stroked on eyes and a hopeful smile. Then dropping the doll face up in her lap, she snatched up yet another handful of straw to make the next one.

Every day for well over a year, the girls and the old woman had all shared the protection of the same tree. Today, like the day before this one and the one before that one, the enormous outreach of the tree's crooked branches shielded them all from the hot sun, as it had from last week's drizzling rain.

Turning their thoughts to their hungry stomachs, the young girls searched each other's faces expectantly. "Who goes first today?" the seven-year-old asked.

"My turn today!" the small five-year-old girl with the curly hair insisted with her usual assertiveness. At their tiny friend's forcefulness, the two older girls exchanged amused glances—not only was she the youngest, but she was so happy to be in the presence of her two older and wiser friends that always she acquiesced. But not today; she *needed* to satisfy her nagging hunger. Without so much as a word of debate, the other two girls conceded, "Okay. Today, *you* go first."

There was something very spiritual about their polite and angelic nature—uncommon for such hungry children, eating what would probably be their only meal for the day. Even more striking was the ceremonial way in which they shared their small bowls of rice and beans and warm corn tortillas. Having determined that the youngest girl would go first, the two older girls set their bowls aside carefully, as their tiniest friend set hers in the center of their circle. Plucking off a piece of her tortilla, the youngest girl dipped into her bowl, scooped up a bite of rice and beans and presented it to the oldest girl. Then the seven-year-old leaned over, tore off a piece of the same tortilla and, holding her dark hair from her face with one hand, pinched up a mouthful of food from the youngest one's bowl, savoring the tasty flavor. Finally, smiling at her friends, the littlest child wiped her hands on her threadbare skirt and took her turn eating her first bite of food for the day from her bowl. They did this, bite by bite, one girl at a time, until the first friend's bowl was empty.

"Who goes next?" came the question when the five-year-old girl's bowl was empty.

"Today, I'm next," the seven-year-old said confidently. And again, the ritual was repeated as the next girl shared her bowl of food with her friends. One bowl at a time, one bite at a time—a strange, and yet reverent, ritual.

Once again a stomach rumbled, and this time its owner shook her head in consternation and slapped her hand over her tummy as if to quiet it. "Shush," she admonished, staring with a frown down at her waist. And then, as if to reassure her little friends that one day all their hunger would end, she pledged, "Some day, when I grow up, I'll send my big shiny car to pick you both up and bring you to my house to eat. We'll live in *town* and have lots of *food!*"

Excited by this prospect, the littlest girl gleefully appealed, "How much? How much?"

"Lots and lots!" answered her friend.

"Tell us! Tell us, Maricella, what we'll have!" she begged. Indulging their imaginations, Maricella quickly obliged. "Oh, we'll have chicken, beef, pork, carnitas, carne asada, tamales and every kind of fruit! And lots of warm tortillas and fresh baked breads and delicious sauces and cheese. And pastries and ice cream. And candies, too!"

"Oh, tell us again! Tell us again about what we'll do when you're rich!" pleaded her friends. Her friends loved Maricella's dreams and didn't deny their friend her grandiose imagination.

"Well," began the impending opulent señorita, sitting up tall, shoulders squared as she straightened her blouse, "when I grow up, I'll have a car." Head held high, she primly patted her face and then her windblown hair, pretending to smooth every strand into place. How she loved telling the story she had told her little friends time and time again, one which served to reinforce her own dreams. "And when I have a car, it will take us to town. . . ."

Perhaps because the sun had now invaded her patch of shade—or perhaps wanting to eavesdrop—the old woman, her fingers as gnarled as the century-old toes of the tree, rustled together a handful of straw, collected her things and moved closer to them. The girls paid no attention.

Now deep in thought, nine-year-old Maricella momentarily closed her eyes and in that blink stepped out of the reality of her life into her fantasy—a dream whose roots were imbedded as deeply as the banyan's.

Nearly a year ago to the day, she had made her first trip the twelve miles on foot with her mother and sisters to the nearest big town, San Miguel. There, standing on a corner of the cobblestone streets where her mother and sisters tried to sell the straw dolls they had made to the tourists passing by, she first saw the children who lived in the town. It was an impression that planted the seeds of her yearning. From that day forward, *town*—as she knew it—became both the foundation and the setting of Maricella's dream.

Looking deep into the eyes of her two friends, Maricella informed them, "The children in town dress in beautiful clothes." Her friends were properly impressed. "So beautiful they shine," she said and, for emphasis, she leaned closer to them and whispered again, "*Shine.*"

As though "shininess," just like cleanliness, was next to godliness, the two little friends repeated slowly, softly, "Shine."

"And *in town* the children eat large burritos with delicious meat and salsas," Maricella continued. With a look of surprise and glee in her eyes she added, "They sit on benches when they eat, *not* on the ground." She motioned from their own spots on the ground to a sweeping imaginary bench in the distance. "And they eat sweets while their mothers hold their hands and take them from store to store."

"Shopping!" her seven-year-old companion burst out gleefully.

"Shopping for what?" the youngest girl asked, listening intently for an answer she'd heard time and time again.

Even so, in anticipation of the words forthcoming, the little girl stopped chewing, her next bite of food held motionless midair, waiting to be savored as much as were Maricella's words.

"Tell us again, Maricella!" the seven-year-old girl demanded on cue.

As though it were so, Maricella replied matter-of-factly, "Well, of course they shop for more shiny clothes, and more sweets."

"Mama gave me sweets on my birthday," the littlest friend piped in.

"But these children eat sweets *all* the time," Maricella clarified. "When I get rich, we will, too!"

"Promise us. Promise we'll always be friends and you'll come for us when you are rich!" her younger friends begged.

"I promise," Maricella nodded solemnly.

"And then we won't *ever* have to go to sleep hungry," said the five-year-old with the beautiful curly dark hair.

"Or wake up hungry," their other friend pointed out.

"No," Maricella assured them authoritatively. "We'll eat delicious meats, and shop in big stores and wear shiny clothes."

"And eat all the sweets we want," the littlest girl craved aloud.

Each wandering into her own reverie, all three girls contemplated this dream. The seven-year-old envisioned the three of them seated around a long table, every inch of it filled with sumptuous food. Her younger friend, unable to comprehend the changes wrought by time's passing, pictured herself in her very own room at Maricella's palace in town, surrounded by store-bought toys, a large bag of candy in her fist. Maricella saw herself stepping from her car, dressed in a white nurse's uniform with bags of shopping purchases under both arms, being greeted by her two children, whose pictures she wore in the gold locket around her neck.

The wind rustled, breaking their trance. "Tell us more. Tell us more," the two younger girls demanded.

"About the nurse?" Maricella probed in a teasing manner, wanting very much to return to her dream and speak the words out loud.

"Oh, yes!" they cried in unison. "Again, Maricella! Tell us about the pretty lady who works in the hospital and owns gold and a car."

"And how you are going to be just like her when you grow up!" the seven-year-old friend coaxed.

The bent tree continued to soak in the sun, buffering three small heads along with an old gray one, as Maricella shared the tale of the nurse, once again solidifying her promise to her friends. Though her dream of being a nurse was planted in town, it was watered by and grew toward fruition because of the charmed faith of the girls' friendship. Gazing out at the world with an open wonder that defied the poverty of their circumstances, the friends listened eagerly as their dark-haired Cinderella detailed—once again—how her life would be transformed, how she would send her gold coach for them, sharing her castle and glass slippers.

When Maricella lived in town, their lives would have a storybook ending as well.

The old woman lay down the doll she was working on and looked skyward. This part of the story usually brought about the longest pause; all three girls, now still, eyes glossy, savored the possibilities in their future.

Suddenly, as though the pumpkin's coach had arrived in the center of town but awaited the arrival of its Cinderella, the two younger girls waited, eyes trained on Maricella. Her impatience born of a need for the plot to go on, the youngest child prompted, "The nurse! Tell us about the nurse!"

Maricella smiled at the prompting. Her thoughts returning to that day, she began, "It was the day Camerina fell." Both of her friends knew this part of the story, too. Nodding sympathetically, they awaited the familiar recounting of the details.

"It was a very hot day," the storyteller continued, "Camerina got very dizzy. She fell, and her head started bleeding! She just lay there, not moving at all. Mama was very scared." Maricella could still picture her mother, kneeling beside her sister Camerina, fretting as she frantically attempted to rouse her young daughter by fanning her and gently dabbing her wound with her striped cotton shawl. "There are many *nice* people in town," Maricella informed her less well-traveled friends. "A man in a good suit stopped in his big car and told Mama to let him take Camerina to the hospital."

"She was crying, so she let the man help, right?" the littlest girl interjected.

"Yes," agreed Maricella. "Mama picked up Camerina and got into the front seat, and me and Letty and Elena sat in the back of the man's very long car." Maricella recalled how she and her sisters had been jostled this way and that as the car bounced, speeding down the narrow cobblestone streets.

"He drove very fast to the hospital. When we got there, they took Camerina and Mama into a room in the hospital, and me and Elena and Letty had to wait for them in another room," she told them, a look of alarm washing anew across her face. Being left alone in the strange surroundings without her mother had been frightening for Maricella. Yet somehow her fear had fastened within her a fierce desire to one day have the means to provide her mama, her sisters and her friends with a sense of safety, as well as all the things she did not have but wanted. "While we were waiting," Maricella said, once again reminding herself of that day's sequence of events, "I looked out the window and saw a beautiful lady who wore a dress so white that it shined."

Conjuring visions of angels in her mind, her five-year-old friend sighed at Maricella's description. "And she was *so* pretty! Right?" the little girl asked with wide-eyed appreciation.

"Yes," smiled Maricella. "The lady wore a white hat with sharp corners—it wasn't like any hat I've ever seen before —and it was pinned to her shiny black hair—beautiful hair." Maricella was reminded of how the woman's hair was curled so that every lock fell back into place as it bounced with her steps when she walked. "She climbed out of a car she drove herself—a shiny blue car," Maricella continued. "She walked straight up the steps and into the hospital, smiling at me when she walked by."

"And she fixed your sister," the youngest child volunteered.

"Yes," agreed Maricella. "The lady in white went into the room to see my sister, and then, after a long time, came back. 'Hello,' she said, 'My name is Connie. I'm your sister's nurse.'" Maricella's voice grew soft and melodious, as she tried to recreate the kind, soft sound of the nurse's voice for her friends. Then, as she remembered how Connie's eyes lingered when they reached hers, Maricella's voice trailed off altogether. Clearly, Maricella had been enchanted by the sweetness and the attention of the nurse.

Maricella was also amazed by the beauty of the gold necklace the nurse wore. "She wore a necklace that sparkled as bright as the stars," Maricella announced with conviction. Maricella's two girlfriends had once again stopped eating, suspended by the glory of the story being told. "It was a big gold heart with shiny red stones around it. 'Do you like my necklace?' she asked me." Maricella smiled at the memory. "Then the nurse leaned closer and opened up the heart to show me a picture of a little girl on one side of it, and she told me, 'She's about your age. She's my daughter. And here is my son. He's younger than you,' and she pointed to the other side of the open gold heart."

The brisk mechanical movements of the old woman's hands halted momentarily. Her eyes moistened as she listened to the description of the children in the locket.

Here Maricella paused, her breath caught in renewed wonder, before she marveled to her companions, "Just think, a beautiful necklace with pictures inside! I'll wear one just like it someday when I'm a nurse."

Perhaps it was the breadth and depth of the growl her stomach emitted rather than the soothing sensation that whirled through her heart when thinking of how wonderful it must feel to help people—like the nurse who had "fixed" her sister—that steered Maricella's thoughts to the shiny car and the gold heart once again. "A nurse is rich enough to buy a shiny car, clean white clothes, and a sparkling necklace," she proclaimed. "I'm going to be a nurse when I grow up!"

The story now over, Maricella looked at the remaining food in the circle and announced with comic grandness, "It's my turn!" A vision of a waiter she had seen when peering onto the patio of a fancy restaurant in town crept into her thoughts. His chest puffed up and back stiff, he served the people at the ornate iron table with such grandeur. Maricella grinned and made a similar regal gesture while replacing the empty bowl in the center of their small circle with her full one. Though unfamiliar with the origins of these gestures, her two little friends chuckled at her antics. Maricella smiled with contentment, offering up her tortilla, saying, "Mama's taking me and my sisters to sell dolls next week. I wish you had dolls to sell so you could come with us."

"Oh, if only we could!" the seven-year-old longed aloud.

"One day, when I'm a nurse in town, you two will come visit me," Maricella consoled them. Mouths full, her friends chewed and chorused a mumbled agreement. They loved her passion, not only because they looked up to and admired this older friend, but because Maricella's dreams held room for them, also. When Maricella became a nurse, their lives—

like that of a butterfly—would metamorphose. They, too, would leave the cocoon of "here" and fly away to "there."

Until then, they joined in the special ritual each day—a sacred feast of food shared selflessly with friends. Perhaps it was the shared dream that united them and made the food so tasty. As one little friend said to the others, "This is my very favorite time of day, here, under *our* bent tree." And the other girls knew that it was so. The rice and beans each shared with the others were somehow the very best they had ever eaten. Not because they tasted better to their mouths, but because they tasted better to their hearts.

Though the girls didn't know it, the old woman had listened to Maricella's story again and again, as she worked silently each day in the shared shade of the old tree. Today, she glanced from the girls—now slipping their sandals back on—to the four finished dolls before her. In the same breath as the breeze whispered through the banyan's leaves, the motherly old woman called out in her age-graveled tone, "Mi hijitas!"

Surprised, the girls looked up at her. The old woman *never* spoke except to greet them hello. "Yes, Nana Chela?" they responded at once, displaying three polite, puzzled smiles. The old woman picked up the dolls she had already completed and held them out toward the girls. "Toma [take]!" she said simply. Though she didn't need to further secure the girls' already riveted attention, she gestured with her arms and head in the direction of the dolls nonetheless, instructing them, nonchalantly yet firmly, to sell them in town.

Momentarily stunned, all three girls stared, jaws slack and eyes wide. "For us?" the two smaller girls questioned. The old woman merely nodded.

Maricella grinned with dawning comprehension, gently shoving her two younger friends toward the old woman, urging, "Go! Now you can come, too!" Their faces bursting into smiling life, the two little girls cried, "Yes! Yes, Nana Chela!" Thrusting the dolls into their thrilled arms, the old woman glanced from one small face to the next—then returned to working on the doll in her lap, suddenly wearing a mask of fierce concentration while performing work that was rote for her.

Perhaps the wise old woman, having witnessed their ritual being repeated day after day—oh so many times— knew Maricella's dream was as good as fulfilled. Perhaps, too, she approved and felt the gift of her dolls would provide an opportunity for the younger girls to create dreams and yearnings of their own. Or, perhaps she had other insights. Or expectations.

The girls were too young, and far too excited, to be so introspective. Awed by the joyful stroke of fate, the girls dashed to return their empty bowls, eager to get home and share the news of their good fortune. Clutching the dream dolls to their chests, they departed down the dusty road toward home, skirts swishing, sandals flopping, hair bouncing and excited chatter—punctuated with squeals of delighted laugher—spilling forth in a deluge of new hopes and anticipation.

"Aye," the old woman sighed softly, her heart now full.

Her eyes darted to the sight of the girls growing smaller and smaller in the distant horizon, then glanced back to the doll under construction in her lap, then back to the girls again. Finally, the little girls faded from her view altogether. Shaking her head, her smile as wide as her bronzed aged face, she mumbled, "Mi hijitas."

Retrieving the gold locket she wore inside her blouse, the old woman opened it and looked at the picture of a little skinny malnourished child on the one side and a young woman clutching a diploma from nursing school on the other. "Mi hijitas," she mumbled. "Mi hijitas."

The Feather That Couldn't Be Found

9

I was a member of a six-person team hired to conduct a national search for a new superintendent of a very large school district in the East—one that had been troubled by ineffectual leadership, damaged by poor fiscal management and plagued by personnel problems. Our team knew the importance of finding the *right* person to get the district back on track.

The search had been unusually lengthy. We had literally scouted the nation for the best and most qualified individual to fill this crucial leadership position. When we completed our search, we had 147 applicants for consideration.

Our committee narrowed this field of applicants first to fifty, then to twenty, then to twelve supremely qualified candidates.

Finally, nearly eight months after we started, we had whittled the list down to the top five finalists—all of whom had extraordinarily stellar credentials. Each of them could do the job required of a superintendent for this district.

Each of the five candidates had been invited to visit with our team. These interviews solidified the candidates' varying standings with each of the committee members.

In our last hours of discussion, we convened with the goal of rating and ranking the finalists. Individual committee members each sought support for the candidate of their choice.

"Dr. Carson is my choice, bar none," said one committee member.

"Dr. Wilson's mine," said another.

"I'm leaning strongly in favor of Dr. Carson myself," said another committee member.

"Me, too," I said. "Three of you with your minds made up for Dr. Carson?" commented one member. "I hope this isn't a sign that the voting is over. Besides," he suspiciously pointed out, "I heard a rumor that Dr. Carson is *gay*."

This happened in the 1980s, a time when social mores were less open to alternative lifestyles than they are today. In many districts, educators who openly admitted to being homosexual were fired (as were other personnel who worked directly with schoolchildren). This rumor, true or not, would attract unwanted press. Both the candidate in question and the district would be put under the microscope of undue scrutiny. Harassment by the media was a sure outcome.

"Oh, my!" sighed one committee member. He quickly shuffled together Dr. Carson's file of resume, references and other employment documents, and turned the folder upside down. "That certainly sheds a different light on this candidate."

"I'll say," said another. "Hiring Dr. Carson would be taking a *very* big risk."

"*Too* big," confirmed yet another committee member as she, too, gathered her copies of Dr. Carson's papers. Leaning forward, she placed his folder in front of her, out of her reach.

Clearing his throat, one committee member pointed out, "We really *don't* know much about his personal life other than he's fifty years old and has never been married. All of the other candidates have children either in public schools or in college. The community always looks more favorably upon those in positions of school leadership who have children of their own."

The same committee member who had made the allegation shifted in his chair and said, "Let me remind this committee that we simply *cannot* bring forward a candidate who is going to be taken to task by the media. This district has been through enough. To hire a person for this position who is even suspect of being gay will only invite problems."

The seed of doubt was planted.

At the end of this session, we rank ordered the top two finalists.

Dr. Carson was not among them.

This incident sadly reminded me of the parable of a man who came to a rabbi and said, "Oh, Rabbi, I have done wrong. I have slandered my friend. I have told lies about him. I have spread rumors. But now I am sorry for what I have done and what I have said. How can I be forgiven?"

The rabbi looked thoughtfully at the man and then said, "Take this feather pillow and go to the town square. Cut the pillow open and let the feathers fly to the wind. That will be your punishment for the ill words you have spoken."

Though quite puzzled by the rabbi's instructions, the man did as he was told. Then he returned to the rabbi and said, "I have done what you told me. Now am I forgiven for slandering my friend?"

The Rabbi replied, "No, you are not forgiven yet. For you have fulfilled only half of your task. First you let the feathers fly to the wind. Now go and collect *every single feather.*"

The moral of this story is that the words we speak have the power to echo far and wide. And, the damage wrought can be irreparable and life changing.

The press did learn of the rumor. Though reporters called it a rumor, they printed it nonetheless. Like scattered feathers in the wind, the information couldn't be retrieved and seriously affected Dr. Carson's career. Four years after that fateful event, Dr. Carson was a candidate in another state for a similar position. A member of the search committee contacted several of our committee members and asked why we hadn't selected him. Two members told them it was because of "the rumor."

I pondered the notion that perhaps the man who shared the rumor about our superintendent candidate should have to collect the "feathers" he spread.

Perhaps he did. Many years later, Dr. Carson applied for the position of director of student admissions at a well-known university. The person who suggested that he apply for the position, and who supported and championed his employment, was the former member of our search committee who started the rumor. Dr. Carson was hired for the position.

Today, Dr. Carson is married and the father of two young children. His wife, a university professor, was coincidentally a member of the search committee that hired him!

10 Many Forms of Love

I'm engaged!

The man I love is what most would call a romantic. As an example, on Valentine's Day, in the grandeur of Boynton Canyon in Sedona, Arizona, he proposed to me—on bended knee, no less! In keeping with the symbolism of this Cupid's day, he slipped an exquisite heart-shaped diamond engagement ring on my finger.

Now that we have new plans for our lives together, we needed to share them with those we love. For me, this meant my family first.

Mine is the sort of family you don't just call up and

announce, "Hi! Guess what? I'm engaged!" So, I flew home
to share the news of my engagement in person. My daughter attends college just an hour and a half from where my
parents live, so I rented a car, picked her up, and together
we drove to the "family home," as it's called. My daughter
is a special little soul mate of mine, so seeing her is always
cause for my heart to sing—that day, even more so! Being
in the car with her for an hour-and-half drive would afford
me the time to share the news of my engagement with her.

When my daughter and I visit my parents, we always
stop at the Eagle Grove Greenhouse and buy a plant for her
grandparents. The ritual in our search for just the *right*
plant is one she and I always enjoy, one that has taken on
distinct and predictable behavior: We hold hands as we
walk up and down the long narrow rows of plants, our
eyes darting at every stalk, bloom and foliage. Should
either of us hesitate for one moment, our eyes meet and are
instantly drawn to the plant in question. Without any
words spoken, somehow we both just *know* when we've
found *the* selection. On this day, we settled on a spectacular
amaryllis, one so bold in its single stalk's bloom of four
gigantic, vibrant orange blossoms striped and edged with
shimmering pearl-white highlights that my daughter first
described it as "eye candy," and then "visual ecstasy."

I paid Mrs. Wilde, the proprietor, and we left. As we carefully placed the beautiful plant in the back seat of the car,
my daughter suddenly burst out with, "Speaking of eye
candy!" Instinctively I knew she had spotted the engagement ring on my finger. The timing seemed right to break
the news, most especially since we had been discussing

"men" and "boys" on the drive—or more succinctly, my fiancé, David (though I had not yet told her of our engagement), as well as the "pro's and con's" of her current boyfriend, with whom she was both happy and frustrated. Allowing the engagement ring to tell the story, I simply held out my hand so that she could see it.

"Oh, Mom," she said tenderly, her beautiful blue-green eyes smiling lovingly. "It's so beautiful. I'm so happy for you." Breaking into laughter, she held up her hand for a "high five" and shouted, "*Yes!*"

And so, without hesitation or reservation, my lovely daughter gave her blessings. Though I knew in my heart that this would be her reaction, I was also relieved. I genuinely wanted her to be happy for me and to feel secure that her room in my heart—and home—was hers for always. She would have a place where she could always come home—one in which her stuffed teddy bears always remained on her bed. Plus, her support would be an invaluable asset as I set out to break the news to my parents and five brothers and sisters (all of whom live within a few miles of each other)!

The flower we selected was received with a great deal of "ooo's" and "awhh's," followed by greetings of hugs, kisses and more hugs. My father set the exquisite plant in the middle of the kitchen table—a table that for more than five decades had listened to morning, noon and evening meal conversations; witnessed the signing of important documents like report cards, insurance policies, and college student loans; and been privy to many a private conversation between parent and child (conversations we children secretly referred to as, 'The come to Jesus meetings'). This regal old family heirloom not only propped up the resplendent blooming amaryllis, it also stood steady as both daughter and granddaughter sat with elbows on it, busy with conversation punctuated with gaiety and laughter. We caught up on the latest activities and events going on in all the lives of this big family. After viewing the latest school pictures and other recent family snapshots now a part of the family photo gallery (the kitchen wall), my daughter began phoning her aunts, uncles and cousins, many of whom would be present that night at a family dinner.

As though my father could read my mind, he asked, "So, what's going on with you, Bob [his nickname for me—I'm the second child and was supposed to be the boy]?" Always interested in the world and its geography, he immediately amended his good-natured questioning with, "You called us last week from Miami, Dallas and Santa Fe. You still living in California, or have you found a new home?"

Laughing, I replied, "Sometimes it *does* feel like I live in an airplane, Dad! But no, I'm still in California. I'm having a great spring. As you know, I'm on tour for my book, plus this is always the busiest time of the year for my consulting business." I thought about adding, "And of course, I'm busy with my fiancé, David," but decided *the parents* weren't quite ready! Dad most especially held the notion that marriage would obliterate the ideal career and lifestyle I've worked to put in place.

Instantly picking up on the idea that I might not have been to my home in a while, my mother said, "Oh, you have to take care of yourself Bobbie [the expanded version of my nickname]. You push yourself too hard. And your house, who's looking after your house? I hope you won't miss out on seeing the daffodils in full bloom. Oh, remember how beautiful they were last year around this time! Who's taking care of your kittens?"

As usual, Dad was most excited by the exterior of my world, my mother the interior. How I loved them! My parents found within themselves an unchanging core to love their children and to care deeply about the goings on in their children's lives—and their grandchildren's lives, and their great-grandchildren's lives, being supportive through thick and thin—sometimes even when we didn't deserve such unconditional benevolence. Being a parent myself, I know firsthand that the actions of children sometimes bring forth untold joy; sometimes untold sorrow—like the year I got divorced. It was a terrible blow to my parents. They worried about me and how the divorce might affect their granddaughter as well as the lives of those surrounding and impacted by the severing of family ties. They feared losing a son-in-law they loved and cared about. Divorce, and everything about it, was counter to a value they long stood for: commitment.

I knew that announcing my engagement would rekindle these concerns and fears. Just as marriage offers connection, the statistics on separation and divorce in today's times paint a dim picture of the likelihood of its survival. As a parent of an adult daughter myself, I knew what my parents might be thinking: *Is this the right decision for her? Will this person she intends to marry accept her for who she is, honor her, commit to creating mutual goals that* preserve the health and life of their love? *Will he like us, accept us, and not take her "away" from us?* I knew that I could expect many tiers of questions from them, each layer getting closer and closer to their feeling of ease about my decision and to feeling that their daughter, their child, had chosen wisely in love.

I considered the crux of my predicament: Though I had made up my mind to marry David, I wanted my family to accept and admire him. In short, their support was important to me.

In my family, when any one of the kids "come home" for a casual visit or holiday, Mom does all the cooking. The rest of us all gather at the kitchen table to talk and reminisce. Sometimes Mom interjects, though mostly she listens and laughs at the things we dredge up about our lives and times. That night, I put on my mother's apron and became a chef by choice! Working closely alongside my mother would give me time to discuss this matter privately, assuage her fears, warm her to the idea, and gain her support. Dad would be the tougher sell. He saw me as self-sufficient and independent—in his eyes, a perfect state. A man in my life would somehow disrupt my life, or in his words, "all that I had going for me." The quicker I could get to Mom's heart, the quicker the route to Dad's seat of reasoning—his head.

"Remember the man I was telling you about the last time I was home?" I asked Mom as we began the meal preparation.

"Chris?" my mother asked. "The one who has been hounding you to get married."

"No. David," I said, feeling a bit disappointed.

"Who?" she asked. "Oh, of course, I remember. You took him to the book awards. And the Chicago keynote. Did he go with you last week when you did the *Geraldo* show?"

"You've got the right one, Mom," I said laughing.

"Naw," Dad said, obviously listening to the conversation from the family room. "You don't want to get married." Soon he and his newspaper sat at the kitchen table.

"I've sent you some pictures, remember?" I asked Dad, realizing my task of persuasion had just doubled.

"I wondered who that was," he replied.

"You're hopeless Dad," I laughed. "Who did you think it was?"

"Oh, I don't know. Donahue, one of those guys," he replied nonchalantly.

"Dad," I said, "Donahue is no longer on television! And, he has silver hair. The man in the photos I sent has dark hair. Plus, in the photos we were standing *very* close together, holding hands. And what about the one where the two of us were sitting on the red rock formation in Sedona? You and Mom visited there just last year, so you know how impossible that would be for me to be there with some talk show host. You can't really believe that was me with Donahue, I mean, what would Marlo think? Really, Dad! Come on, you're joking with me, right?"

"Oh," is all he said. He continued reading the paper.

"Where are those photos, Dad?" I asked.

"Oh, I'm not sure. They're around here somewhere," he replied. And then he asked my mother, "Mom, what did you do with those photos?"

I knew that if the photos had made it into my mother's hands, they'd be on the family wall where there is no less than 12 zillion photos of their six children and the families they've spawned, some pet photos included. I quickly scanned the wall. Not one of the new photos I'd sent of my David was there.

"Mom and Dad," I said softly, "though I've enjoyed every single minute of the glorious years I've been single, it's unlikely that I'll want to be single forever."

"Well, you should," Dad said matter-of-factly. "You have everything you need."

"And we still love Dic," my mother interjected. "He'll always be our son-in-law."

Defending myself, I gently countered, "Yes, I think that's as it should be, but I want you to know that David is some-one very special, too." I hesitated, and then said, "He's asked me to marry him." I stopped with that, and looked at each of them to see how they were taking this. There appeared to be no change in their relaxed demeanor, so I added, "And I've said 'yes.'"

A very long silence followed, and finally, with a frown of dismay on her face, my Mother asked, "*Why* would you do that?" As if genuinely baffled, she itemized reasons why I might want to reconsider: "You have been so happy on your own, not having to answer to anyone, not having to adapt to someone else's schedule, not having to cook and clean for anyone, not having anyone else interfering with the things you want to do or when you want to do them, not having to rearrange your schedule for someone else, not having to defer your goals to the goals of someone else . . . "

"Really?" my father questioned. "What does he do? Does he make any money? Does he . . . has he . . . ?"

This continued until the dinner hour when all of my siblings and their children convened at which pointed it continued—en masse!

Arriving first, my brother Mark greeted me with, "Well, I hear another good woman bites the dust!" Several steps behind him, his wife, Debbie, called, "Let's see the ring!"

Kevin and Peggy and their four children came in next. "Congratulations!" Kevin said, grinning from ear to ear. "I hear we're getting help with our spring planting from a guy in California. We'll let him take the graveyard planting shift and see if he's worth his salt!"

"Oh, no!" his wife Peggy chimed in. "That would be far too easy." Looking at four children—ages five, seven, nine, and twelve—she said, "Kevin, remember that vacation we've been talking about, you know, the one *without* the kids. Let's let David stay with the kids and if he still wants in the family after that, by all means we'll have him!"

I knew their razzing would continue, and that, alas, I would have to take it good naturedly. Even so, I was beginning to wonder why I hadn't just put everything I wanted to say in a letter and let them all get used to it on their own time. Of course, it's not the way things are done in my family. Besides, there *is* a point to scrutinizing the new in-law. After all, in our family it is, as my mother once said, "a new person to love." Well, okay, what she actually said was, "a new person to get used to!"

By now most of the family had arrived, and though some of the members of my family had met David, most of them had not, so I brought photos—those carefully screened to present him in the best of light. Feeling as if I was presenting evidence for the defense, I displayed "Exhibits A through G."

"Oh," said one brother, perhaps a bit surprised. "He's quite a bit older than you!"

"No," I remarked. "There's only five or six years between us."

"He looks too old for you!" came his response.

"Well, we kids just have the benefit of great genes. Our parents have always looked ten years younger than they are, so do we kids!" I remarked, trying to calm myself from feeling defensive.

"Where's he *from?*" Mark, my oldest brother, asked.

"How long have you known him? Exactly?" came a question from another brother. Looking around the table, he added, "I think we should have him send a resume, a financial statement and a background check—what do you guys think?" This he asked in a joking manner—or at least I think he was joking!

"We've celebrated our year-and-a-half anniversary," I replied.

"Only that?" my sister asked with raised eyebrows. "You went out with that last man for three years. He asked you to marry him. What was *wrong* with him?"

"You don't marry every man you have a relationship with!" I countered. "The other guy was terrific, but he was more of a . . . you know . . . a relationship—someone to go out with. David is much different; he's a keeper. We have everything in common. He's very exciting and a lot of fun.

And with him in my life, it just seems as if everything has more meaning. When he asked me to marry him, I couldn't think of one reason not to. Saying yes was easy and natural. My heart *knows* that *this* man is for me."

Perhaps feeling a bit of sympathy for my having to "justify" my choice of love—or perhaps it was that the photos had just now finally reached her—a sister-in-law assessed the photos of my fiancé and remarked, "He's really tall. Looks fit. Quite handsome!"

"Really, really, handsome," confirmed another sister-in-law, looking at her husband and then playfully teasing him about the size of my engagement ring, "Lets, see," she said, "how many days until the next Valentine's Day? Time to start saving up, I say. It's only eleven months away!"

"This is really boring," said my twenty-one-year-old daughter who was experiencing a different brand of love with a new boyfriend. "I can't believe I'm sitting here. It's Friday night! Tell me what other girl, with the best-looking *new* boyfriend in the world, two days before my birthday no less, would want to be sitting at a dinner table—with relatives—discussing her mother's engagement? Why don't we just vote on the guy so we can get on with this! I vote 'yes.' Can I be excused now?"

My dear daughter, while happy for me, was in a particularly bad mood because the object of her affection was an hour and a half away. Young, restless and feeling insecure about the depth of what she and he shared—or as she so aptly put it, "he's the type that 'when the cat's away, the mouse will play!'"—she wanted to be with her boyfriend and not here with us.

As trying as this moment was, I knew that in our family screening the prospective applicant is much more than a hazing. Two questions posed by one of my brothers are telling because they reveal how protective a loving family is of each other: "Does he appreciate you?" "Does he know how special you are?" I thought the questions were very loving. And I knew the answer to both was yes.

As I looked around the room at my family, I realized how special they were, and how much I appreciated them. And I saw the evidence of genuine love—many forms of it— everywhere. I glanced first at my parents, husband and wife for nearly fifty-three years now. They knew every nuance of the other. Dad, pointing to the amaryllis in the middle of the table, was telling my sister of the amaryllis he discovered "jetting up from the earth" in my Great Old Auntie Hilda's 160-year-old backyard, and how he observed it day after day, hoping it might bloom in time for Valentine's Day so he could present it to my mother, his wife and sweetheart. The plant obliged, blooming on cue. So, on the day that Cupid reserves to send his arrows to the hearts of lovers, my father waited for just the right moment to surprise my mother, his love, with the star of Holland— an amaryllis with deep crimson, velvety petals and white starry centers. The opportunity presented itself when she went to town for groceries that day. While she was gone, he picked the exquisite flower and placed it along with a love note in the refrigerator where he knew she would find it. Obviously, he felt this was more special than simply handing it to her, or just putting it in a vase with water and setting it on the table.

As he had anticipated, when my mother returned from her shopping and began putting items in the refrigerator, she discovered the beautiful flower and his note. At this point in the conversation, as though it were a well-rehearsed script, my mother took over telling the story. As it goes, right after she discovered my father's gesture, she looked up, and there stood my father, like a schoolboy, waiting in anticipation with an ear-to-ear smile, eager to see her reaction. He held both his hands behind his back, a sign my mother took to mean that he was hiding something in them. When she smiled knowingly, and asked him what he was up to, he produced a heart-shaped box of chocolates. While endearing, this is also quite an interesting gift for my father to give her because after living together for five-plus decades, my father *knows* that my mother does not like chocolate—and so the chocolates become his. Yet, year after year, he continues to buy chocolates "for her"! Theirs is a love rooted in passion, honor, commitment—and supreme attachment to their six children, all of whom adore, respect and honor them.

Next, my attention turned to my brother as he leaned over to his seventeen-month-old son who sat in a high chair next to him, wiping his little boy's face with a napkin. He gently rubbed the baby's fine blond curls and kissed him on the head. His gesture was so natural, demonstrating clearly his great paternal love, making it clear that a kiss is the *language* of the heart. His wife, seated beside them, her hand on my brother's knee, smiled with a soft serene delight at her husband and son, her love for them apparent.

Across the table, another brother and his wife of twenty

years playfully joked and laughed intimately with each other, oblivious to the "noise factor" from all of us now involved in individual and separate conversations. Yet another brother and his wife, watching their five-year-old try to force a fork into his mouth that was loaded with more food than could possibly fit, looked at each other, their hands over their mouths, trying to stifle their laughter so their son wouldn't think they approved. My daughter, Jen, who had slipped away from the table, sat huddled in the corner on the phone, her whispered conversation punctuated with occasional giggles. She was experiencing yet another sort of love, perhaps not as stable or as deep, but probably as intense as any other at the moment.

My siblings and their spouses were people who genuinely liked each other, people who believed in themselves and each other. As importantly, this was a family who knew of love. As I looked at them, I was warmed at the idea of sharing love as they knew it, and became even more sure that I wanted to marry David.

Mom must have been reading my mind. She smiled knowingly.

One by one, they acquiesced. Though I knew that it was because each now felt comfortable that I was with someone who shared the value of love as *this* family understood and practiced it, I asked them what had been the deciding factor.

My father, who, of course, values the protector and protective nature of love, said, "Oh, I guess it was when you said he makes certain to lock up the doors and to turn on the alarm at night, and when you said he keeps his word and pays his way, that's when I knew he's a 'real man.'"

My mother told me, "When you said that he has family and frequently calls or visits them, I knew that he wouldn't prevent you from staying close to us and that would always be a priority for you, as it is now. And when you told me that he deeply cares for and still financially supports his stepfather, I knew he was a compassionate man and that he would care for you. It sounds as though he's a caretaker. He sounds secure enough in himself to value your relationship with your family, and has introduced you to the members of his family." Concluding with her maternal confidence, she added, "Then, when you said that you would care for him, no matter what and for always and in all circumstances, I knew that he had gained your trust and your love, and surely he must be worthy."

"When you said you share the same values and spiritual beliefs, and that you worshipped together," one brother said, "that's when I decided he was a man you would be safe having for a husband."

Said one sister, "I figured it was going to go well when I learned that he loved your kittens and brought them food from restaurants and bought them tuna fish. I knew that would find a home in your heart! A guy that loves animals has got to be a good guy!"

One brother added, "When I saw the two of you together that evening when we went to dinner when I was in San Diego, I just knew it was right for you—that he's right for you. When you parted, he told you to drive safely. And then you kissed him. And in that kiss I saw a love story."

Her marital content bubbling forth as a desire for everyone she loved to know the same experience, his wife said,

"I can see how happy you are. If he makes you *this* happy, then it must be right for you."

"He sure is handsome," one sister-in-law sanctioned primly, then broke into an approving smile and added, "and when you said that his being in your life colors everything in a loving and positive way, I knew that our vote was just a rubber stamp. You found someone you want to be with, your mind is made up!"

And so it is, that we *voted* David into the family. A family with an enormous capacity to love each of the souls they call "family"—one in which David is now welcomed. Such is the nature of the taste berry of love.

Now, if *he'll* have *them*. . . .

11

Deliberate Design of Two

A gray African goose stood at the rear of my father's truck, staring into the wide chrome bumper—completely engrossed with the image he saw there. The goose preened, cocking his outstretched neck from side to side, occasionally flapping his wings to punctuate his conversation of clucks and honks. It was an interesting and amusing sight!

When I noticed that the goose was still there nearly four hours later, I thought it was odd. Never having seen such curious behavior from a goose, I asked my father about it.

"Dad," I said, "that old gray goose has been standing beside your truck all day. Do you have any idea why?"

"Oh, sure," he answered without hesitation. "That's Grady. He lost his 'missus' a year ago, and he's lonely without her. For nearly a month he searched the farmstead for her every day. Then one day, as he passed the shiny bumper, he caught sight of his reflection in it. I guess he thinks he's found her." Dad chuckled at the bird's solution and then added, "So every day he comes to be with her. At least I'm fairly sure he thinks he's coming to be with her— either that or he's in love with himself!"

It's not like the goose is alone in the world. There are ten other geese on the farm. Each and every night my father diligently puts all the geese in their "hen house" to assure that the foxes nearby don't make them their evening meal. Each and every morning, the geese wait impatiently at the door of their protective shed for my father to free them so they can roam the farmstead. When Grady is turned loose, he departs from the others, preferring instead to be with "his missus." On a full waddle, he rushes to wherever my father's truck is parked and stares into the truck's shiny silver bumper and exuberantly cackles away, perhaps filling her in on the events that transpired while they were apart.

"Isn't it a bit strange that Grady stays at the bumper *all* day long?" I asked my father.

"Not if that's where he thinks his companion is," my father replied. "He's devoted to her."

I was intrigued by the apparent affection this goose had once shared with his mate, an affection so strong he was determined to hang on to some semblance of it after her parting. "Dad," I asked with genuine curiosity, "Why do you think that goose would go to such lengths?"

"No mystery to it," he said matter-of-factly. "Everything in nature is a *deliberate design of two*. It's natural to want a companion. Union, having someone to share your days with, being concerned with someone other than yourself, gives reason to life." He looked from Grady—busy interacting with at least the memory of his "missus"—to the other geese, all strolling in pairs about the farm, and said, "Most all of us seek a mate—even after painful loss and heartbreak in that quest."

His words struck me as especially loving and insightful, reminding me that in our greatest joys and sorrows, we generally reach out for the person with whom we are closest to share the experience. And it's this sharing that exponentially heightens the experience. When my daughter was born, as overjoyed as I felt, the experience was incomplete until I saw the joy in her father's eyes. This past week my daughter, now grown, came to visit me. As she handed me a bouquet of flowers, she watched intently for my reaction. When I swooned at the beauty of the flowers—and her gesture of giving them to me—her eyes lit up and a beautiful ear-to-ear smile appeared. Buying the flowers for me had elicited her joy, but seeing my happiness in receiving them had made her joy complete.

My father paused, looked toward the sky and summed it up with his words, "A sunset watched with your mother is much more beautiful than one I see without her."

Later that day, two of my brothers stopped at the farm to visit me before I caught a flight to return to my home. Grady was still attending to his lover in the bumper, so I asked my brothers what they thought about the goose's behavior. It seemed just as natural to them as it had to my father.

"What an exceptional pair *those two* are!" said my brother, Tim, laughing as he watched Grady in the company of his own reflection. "They *still* have a love affair going on!"

"What do you make of it, Tim?" I asked pointing to the goose.

"Oh," he said, "you see that kind of behavior all the time in nature. Besides, that hen was Grady's best friend, his foraging partner. They swam in the pond together. He protected her from predators—real or imagined. You should have seen the way he'd chase off the dog—honking, hissing, flapping—if the dog got too close to the hen. She was Grady's soul mate. As you can see, poor old soul, he sure misses her!" His comment struck me as appropriate from a man who some years back had picked a biblical verse for his wedding program cover that read, "I will give them one heart."

"That reminds me of a story a friend once told me," I replied. "A pair of geese were migrating to the islands in the Straits of Magellan. The female had broken her wing and, unable to fly, was making the migration south by foot. While she marched steadily southward, the male flew overhead a short distance, then turned back to rejoin his mate. The male refused to abandon his partner. He chose to remain her loyal companion—even if it meant ignoring his age-old instinct to fly away with the migrating flock. Grady must feel that same attachment."

"Grady does miss his mate," my brother Mark agreed. "It reminds me of the scene I witnessed early one morning last November when driving to work. A doe had been hit by a car and lay by the side of the road. I stopped to see if by chance she might still be alive. When I got out of the car, I heard a rustle in the bushes nearby. There stood a large six-point buck, waiting me out, no doubt against every instinct warning him to run off.

"The doe was dead. As I pulled away, from my rearview mirror I saw the buck emerge from the bushes, walk over to the doe, sniff around her face and nudge her as if he expected her to get up and go into the woods with him. Every few seconds he'd look up, as if on alert for danger, and then turn his attention back to the doe. I decided to pull over and observe for a few minutes. Every half minute or so the buck would retreat to the trees nearby, only to emerge again and try to coax the doe to get up.

"On the way home that evening, when I approached the same area where I had seen the deer that morning, sure enough, the buck was still keeping guard over the doe. I stopped to watch. The buck repeated essentially the same behavior I'd seen earlier. But now, with dusk upon him, the buck—perhaps finally resigned that the doe was dead— flung his head into the air, snorted and then bounded off into the woods. He couldn't quite bring himself to leave until the danger of darkness became too great!

"It's been my experience that many species in the animal kingdom seek union and mourn its loss. In a paired union, the loss of a mate can be so great that, like people, heart-broken with grief over one partner's death, the other part-ner loses his will to live. Sometimes that happens in nature, as well. Old Grady didn't come to that conclusion. He set about finding his companion."

But eventually Grady did come to that conclusion. Ten months after my visit home, my parents traded the old truck in for a car, a vehicle more conducive to spending time together taking drives in comfort—perhaps to share the beauty of watching the sunset from places other than their own porch.

"Dad," I asked, "what does Grady think of the bumper on the new car?"

"Oh," he replied, "the bumper on the new car is painted fiberglass. It doesn't shine. Without the shiny bumper, Grady lost his missus once again. He spent nearly a week looking for her all over the farm. He nearly drove us crazy with his honking and calling out to her. He looked behind every bush and building on the place, but to no avail. He couldn't find her anywhere."

"Did Grady join the other geese, then?" I asked.

"No," my father said, sounding forlorn. "Grady mourned for several days. Then he died—just eight days after we traded in the truck."

The bonds of sharing—perhaps interwoven into all souls—sweeten life's joys, ease the bitterness of its losses . . . and color the beauty of sunsets shared.

12

Of Lilacs and Springtime

This past April while visiting my parents on the farm I'd grown up on, I wandered outside to drink in the feel of "home"—a comfort I really needed right then. I was used to sunny Southern California mornings, and the brisk early-morning Iowa air nipped at my nose, ears and bare hands. With my father's fleece-lined jacket wrapped around me, and my hands snuggled deep in its well-worn pockets, I meandered around the spacious homestead— when the unexpected sweet scent of lilacs suddenly called to me. Turning toward the bountiful hedge of lilacs in the distance, I spotted what looked like blooms. I hurried over.

The lavender lilacs were indeed in glorious bloom! I pulled a plentiful clump to my face and inhaled the intoxicating scent, as I had done every springtime throughout my childhood. A warm delight seeped through my chilled bones, and I smiled at the thought that spring had arrived! Strolling back to the house, the promise of springtime—warmth, renewal and beauty—journeyed right along with me.

My father sat at the kitchen table, poring over the morning market reports. "It's spring! The lilacs are in bloom!" I joyously announced.

"Lilacs in bloom or not, it isn't spring until winter's gone," he contradicted. "We'll get a bit of cold weather yet."

But my heart refused to let the optimism that the lilacs had brought to me fade. Immediately, I recalled the card my mother had sent me just that past week—one that had subconsciously inspired this trip home. My mother knew that I was feeling down. On the cover of the card she sent me was a photo of a single flower emerging from a desolate barren slope of rock. The exquisite flower *willed* itself to have life, in spite of the conditions around it. Inside were the words "In the midst of winter, I found within me an eternal spring," followed by my mother's words: "Spring has always been your favorite time of year. As always, it's *within*."

These are words that my mother, ever the optimist, lives by. Even in the midst of winter, she finds spring.

"It's pouring rain!" Dad once said.

"Everything smells so fresh after a rain!" Mom responded.

"But I'd wanted to get the yards mowed today," he replied, obviously disappointed.

"We need the rain," she countered. "Now everything will be greener."

"But the forecast is rain for the entire day," Dad moaned.

"Then we should go to the movies this afternoon," Mom smiled.

"It's so expensive," he retorted.

"That's precisely why we should go the matinee," she countered. "Three of the kids can get in free, and it's only half-price for the rest of us."

Recalling this Rockwell scene of a Sunday afternoon when I was twelve, I'm reminded that for my mother torrential rains produced a rainbow, and there was always a pot of gold at the end of it. I love her sense of joy and optimism.

And her ever-ready willingness to share it.

Throughout my childhood and over the course of my adult years, when I met with success, my mother presented me with a bouquet of lilacs. And on the days when the lemons were so bitter they simply couldn't be made into lemonade, no matter how much sugar was added—like the day a good friend passed away; like the day when a long-standing love relationship ended; like the day I moved from a home I enjoyed into a different one because of my spouse's new employment; like the day . . . like the day . . . like the day—lilacs arrived from my mother with a note of understanding to match their beauty and sweet fragrance. "Spring has always been your favorite time of year," she always reminded. "As always, it's *within*."

Even so, it was the lilacs that made her words ring true.

With the sight and fragrance of that April morning's lilacs came the realization of why a trip home was necessary. I needed to assuage my sadness, my feelings of loneliness, my melancholy. I was pining. My dear daughter, now an adult, had moved from my home into a place of her own. She now lives many states and many miles away. While happy for her, I mourn the loss of her nearness. When I opened the door to allow my beautiful butterfly to go into the world, a winter breeze filled her now empty room—one where once the sound of her music, her chatter, her laughter, the smell of her sweet perfume (and her dirty cowboy boots) sprang forth.

That morning, the sight of the lilacs brought my mother's words back to life. They reminded me that in the midst of an internal winter, a winter that is *within*, I must recall the beauty of springtime and scent of the lilacs it brings. As I gaze upon the two-decades worth of teddy bears that still sit upon my daughter's now-empty bed, I vow I will not see her as having gone away, but rather as taking part in new and wondrous experiences in a world that has as many springtimes as winters. One in which lilacs grow in abundance.

"Dad, the lilacs are in bloom. It's spring!" I assured my father that day.

"Hmm," he said, glancing at me, his expression skeptical. Noting my frown, his features softened. "Of course it's possible that spring has arrived," he placated, smiling. "After all, like you said, the lilacs are in bloom."

The next morning I bundled up in warm clothes. It was snowing outside.

"Snow," said my father, his gentle version of "I told you so." "Guess old man winter isn't ready to leave us quite yet."

"Speak not to me of winter," I said. "The lilacs are in bloom. It's spring."

Oh, for the ever-renewing taste berry of the beauty of springtime! And the sweet and irrepressible scent of the lilacs to remind us that spring is also found *within*.

13   Love Owed

He was an American from Texas. She was a kitty from Manila. Makati, Manila. Actually, she wasn't from anywhere. The last and smallest of four kittens born to a stray feline who could barely attend to her own day-to-day survival, the kitten and her siblings were abandoned within weeks of their birth.

He had abandonment issues of his own. Tall, handsome and high profile—and paying a price for professional success—he was away on business yet again, a long way from home, and alone.

Though neither kitten nor man was aware of it at the

time, theirs was a fate of each heart yearning for what they once had, but had no longer. Fate would be kind; providence had assigned man and kitten intersecting paths.

For the first two weeks of their mother's absence, the scraggly little orphans searched for food by day. With each and every approaching sunset, they returned to their birthplace for the night. Huddling for comfort and snuggling for warmth, three gray-haired little brothers and one tiny butterscotch-colored sister piled themselves on top of one another, forming a lumpy clump of breathing fur.

As time went on, their search for food, fun and frolic took them closer and closer to the horizon, and farther and farther away from home—and each other. On a particular day like any other, one particular little gray brother didn't return home—not that night, or any night thereafter. Some days later, a second brother disappeared and, a week later, the third. Just like that, Manila Kitty no longer knew of the whereabouts of her brothers—nor even if they were still alive.

At just three months of age, Manila Kitty was alone in the world.

She'd been wandering from neighborhood to neighborhood for nearly a month when a little girl on her way home from school spotted Manila Kitty and gleefully chirped, "A kitty! Here, kitty, kitty!" In an effort to discern the little girl's intentions, Manila Kitty, like a robin watching a worm, cocked her head and stared imperceptibly in her direction. The child crouched down, extending an open hand, and once again summoned, "Here, kitty, kitty." It was a sweet melodious tone, unadulterated, void of malice, innocent. Manila Kitty was interested in learning more. The little person set down her lunchbox, opened it, reached inside and in a sing-song voice invited the young cat, "C'mon, kitty, come and get it." Manila Kitty slyly sidled up a little closer to inspect the child's offering. Coaxing the kitten into giving up her apprehension, the little girl tore a piece of moist bread from the remains of a sandwich and tossed it in the cat's direction. Instantly, Manila Kitty leaped on it and in one swallow gulped it down. A second piece was tossed and fell a little closer to the child. Enticed by the first tasty morsel, Manila Kitty, ever so watchful, tip-toed closer, snatched it up and, once again, devoured it. Yet a third piece was released—this time falling directly on top of the little girl's well-worn tennis shoe! This was going to be even more tricky, but Manila Kitty was up to the effort!

Planting her feet firmly, Manila Kitty slowly and cautiously stretched her body forward as far as it would go. But the scrap of bread was still several inches out of reach. Edging closer, the cat slithered her right front leg forward and, claws extended, hooked the bread and plucked it into her watering mouth!

The little girl was even quicker! In one fell swoop, Manila Kitty was scooped up into her arms where her seven-year-old hands with intent, chubby fingers began vigorously rubbing, brushing and stroking Manila Kitty's spiny frame. Though their touch was clumsy and far from gentle, the stimulation of the little girl's fingers felt good. Manila Kitty decided she'd tolerate this joyful pummeling.

There was more to come. As though she were a doll, the little girl rocked Manila Kitty to and fro in her arms. She cuddled her tight against her chest, pressing her face, neck and hair into the little cat. The little girl then held the kitten up so they were nose to nose, and chattered and crooned. And though she was not without reservation about all this, Manila Kitty liked the little girl's devoted attention.

The little girl seemed to know of Manila Kitty's insecurity. As quickly and swiftly as she'd picked the kitten up, she set Manila Kitty back on the sidewalk and picked up her books and lunchbox. Then, singing, "Here, kitty, kitty. Here, kitty, kitty," she began walking.

Manila Kitty followed—all the way home.

Home. Safe, warm and content, Manila Kitty fell peacefully asleep, wrapped lovingly by the little girl in a soft cotton towel placed inside a makeshift box. It was, perhaps, a good world after all.

Unfortunately, her good fortune didn't last. Through the same door the little girl had unlocked by removing a key that hung on a chain from around her neck, Manila Kitty was put out. And on the same day! Gone was the little girl's joyful voice . . . a source of food . . . a warm house that smelled good . . . a reprieve from barking, chasing dogs. Manila Kitty once again knew the contempt of people who had no sympathy for a malnourished little kitty with a country, but without a home.

Every day for a week, Manila Kitty returned to the little girl's porch each morning and each night in hopes of catching a glimpse of the little person who had shared lap time with her. No one came, though once the little girl had placed a small bowl of milk around the corner of the house. When the same big people discovered it—those people who demanded Manila Kitty's departure—the charity abruptly stopped.

Once again in exile, Manila Kitty, the vagabond, resumed wandering from neighborhood to neighborhood, each territory seemingly as hostile as the next.

Day after day, the routine remained the same: search for food, shelter and safety. Owls lurked, hawks hovered, jeepneys (Manila jeeps) rarely if ever swerved, dogs sniffed her out, humans chased her away. Two-legged monsters in caps, denim jeans and sneakers skipped rocks off her back and snatched her up by the tail. Women shooed her away when she ransacked their garbage cans while foraging for food. They shook towels and newspapers at her when she romped with their well-groomed, flealess felines—those cats who possessed calm eyes, silky fur and fancy collars with telephone numbers, those whose food came in expensive packaging and was eaten from bowls with cat names on them. Men yelled and sometimes threw objects. Just last week, Manila Kitty received a painful, swift kick from the man who, while starting his car, discovered that she had spent the night sleeping on the roof of it.

Homeless, hungry, sleep deprived—and now wounded —Manila Kitty's plight was that of abandonment and deprivation. But there were yet other demons to be propitiated. Nightmares came by day as well as by night. *What becomes of a little kitty who has no mother, father, sister, brother or companion?* she thought. She desperately missed her mother, even if her mother had already fulfilled her role by performing the necessary rite that allowed the kitten's spirit to enter the world. And where had her brothers—her playmates—gone? Why had they not come back for her? Sometimes, on those days when hunger consumed her, Manila Kitty would see—just over there on the other side of the street—a vision of one of them. But always the phantom sighting turned out to be just another stray cat, one not at all interested in friendship and, quite often, very interested in ferociously guarding its territory.

Still, she preferred melancholy to desperation. An angry world had taken its toll. Yet sticks and stones and bruises and abrasions—and the bone-cracking kick—aside, it was the lack of devotion, attachment and loving contact that Manila Kitty considered the biggest assault of all. She clung tenaciously to her hope of once again finding connection with a loving spirit somewhere in the world.

To comfort herself, she licked her right front paw, lowered her head, closed her eyes, and made long slow swipes with the moistened paw across her face and then around it. This she did several times, leaning into the strokes, tilting her head this way then that in an effort to satisfy her longings. When it seemed not to offer the solace she sought, she tried to work up a purr instead. When gratification from the tone of her trill seemed yet again fleeting, she resorted to dragging her injured body back and forth, back and forth, across the base of the shrub that was now her "home."

Forsaken, the meow she cried was one of rebellion: *Why had her guardian angel chosen such an ungracious destiny?*

The faint meow in the distance was an intrusive one. At first the man thought of passing it by, but its indigent nature beckoned, begged. Closer now, he realized that the sound was coming from beneath the little bush just to the right of the sidewalk. The American on business in Manila crouched down to get a better look. When his eyes adjusted to the darkness, the delicate form of a scrawny shivering cat appeared. "A cat!" he declared matter-of-factly. "It's a little itty-bitty kitty." In a comforting tone he informed her, "That's a pretty panicky cry from such a little thing. Sounds like you've got a problem." Then he asked her, "Do you have a problem, kitty?"

Hungry, cold and so internally injured that she could do little more than stand her ground—and now confronted by a six-foot-two-inch giant—Manila Kitty was instantly skeptical. He was several stories tall, and she was all but unnoticeable. Playing an act of daunting opponent, she drew back, stiffened her legs, arched her back, puffed her fur and hissed with authority. He understood body language, too. "Oh, I won't hurt you," he soothed. When she offered fright without flight, he reached out his hand ever so slowly, saying, "Such a little kitty should be at home. Why aren't you home?"

Home. That's where he wanted to be. He remembered "home" then, and compared it to the "homes" where he found himself now. The walls that constantly surrounded him were those of one hotel room or another; the people temporary others. It all added up to intimate isolation. Somehow the priorities of his life now seemed askew.

Once home had been a place where wife, children and pets blurred into a mixture of love and laughter, balancing time between work and family. He wondered why he had allowed himself to take them for granted, why he hadn't spent as much time with them as with his business colleagues, why he had seen family as a liability, a "consuming responsibility." And so he had lost them.

How he would love to have those assets now. The noisy children had grown up and were parents themselves. Still so angry over how he deprived them of his love, they left him alone and rarely if ever returned his calls. Much the same as the women did. When they could no longer tolerate his emotional illiteracy, each woman in turn had fired him from the job of being her partner. Events went on without him, even friendships were defined more by the situation at hand than by their depth of interest in him. Praise unspoken, love missed, time away—all had created a large chasm between what he once didn't need and now did. How had he let so much precious time slip away . . . let them slip away?

The urgency of the cat's meow snapped him out of his contemplation and back to her plight. He observed her in silence: *What does she need? What should I do with her?*

Manila Kitty had questions of her own: *Is he an enemy? What are his intentions?* He understood the language of negotiation and waited her out. The cat scrutinized his repose, sternly keeping in sight the huge "paws" of the man who had walked by her bush home three days in a row. Momentarily feeling that it was perhaps she, and not he, who was in charge—or maybe the pangs of hunger gnawed in her belly—Manila Kitty decided she would bring closure to their silent assessment of one another. She relaxed her body and lifted her mournful gold eyes to his brown ones.

Apparently, he could read her mind, too. "You're hungry, aren't you?" he asked, "How long has it been since you've had food?" She found no reason to judge him harshly any longer. She meowed beseechingly. "I see," he said. "Okay, then. I won't be long."

The man returned with a small can of tuna fish. Crouching down, head and shoulders practically beneath the bush with her, his large hands grappled with the ring at the top of the can and then peeled it open. "Mmm, taste this," he coaxed. He gingerly tossed the sharp-edged lid aside, and held the can out to her so she could smell it. Then he set it on the ground carefully and slowly slid the can closer and closer to her. Pursuing friendship, he softened his tone and remarked, "Looks like you've been under the bush for some time, kitty. You making this your home, or are you just lost?" Manila Kitty was far too needy to keep up her defenses. In a slow, laborious gesture, she leaned her head in the direction of his hand.

"C'mon over here, then," he said. "I won't bite. You can walk, can't you?" he asked her, and then added, "Are you hurt?" She didn't even bother to look at him and instead gulped her food. He wondered if she tasted it. But it wasn't the food that inspired her haste, rather it was the craving in the pit of her stomach that food simply couldn't assuage. She wanted the food to be sure, but needed the touch of his hand even more. Slowly he lifted his hand over her head and lowered it mindfully, scratching her head lightly, his fingers moving gently from the top of her head, behind both ears and over her thin little body. So desperate for *that* touch, Manila Kitty freely gave in to his caregiving.

For the next two days, around the same time, American Man appeared with a piece of leftover meat from his dinner. One evening as he knelt beside Manila Kitty while she ate, it occurred to him that she greatly needed a bath—or at least that was his rationale for removing her from the dangers of being alone and "on the streets." "Kitty," he announced, "I'm taking you home for a bath."

She knew not of his rank, powers or his spheres of influence. Nevertheless, she offered no resistance when he cautiously picked her up and carefully tucked her in his arm for the trip to his hotel room three blocks away. There he bathed her. The warmth of the man's gentle touch ameliorated the pain she felt as his hand came in contact with her side. He wrapped her in a towel and set her in the corner of the couch, fluffing and tucking pillows on each side of her. "This should make you feel better," he announced. As he went about his business in preparation for his next workday, she lay cradled in her little nest of pillows, her eyes escorting his every move.

When he crawled into bed and turned off the last of the lights, Manila Kitty decided she was no longer content to be on the couch, no matter how comfortable it was. She meowed defiantly. He flicked on the bedside light in response and, noting her wince, knew she was in great pain. He got up and brought the cat to his bed, laying the little kitten near him as he settled back into the covers. She waited until he lay still and then, crawling to where his hands rested, tunneled her small head beneath his large hand in a most determined motion, one that petitioned,

"Rub me, pet me, caress me. Now!" When his response was placating but halfhearted, Manila Kitty burrowed her head into his hand again, this time leaning the whole of her force into her movements, which demanded, "Stroke me!"

"Okay, okay!" chuckled American Man. As if he understood her yearning—or was placating his own—he chided, "Such a restless heart, kitty! Such impatience!" Whispering tenderly, he questioned, "What do you need? Hmmm? Are you all alone in the world—like me? Hmmm? Have you ended up too short on love—like me?"

The words, while directed at the kitty, boomeranged; it felt to him as if his own soul were being interrogated. He wasn't sure if the ache in his heart was for the wounds of the cat or for his own. But the truth refused to be ignored and so roared, *Life is precious. Time is short. Love is all there is.* Stirred by this impassioned insight—and bound by a desire to move beyond an aloneness that he now found insufferable—he vigorously stroked the kitten, even though she was asleep and demanded it no more.

He talked to her anyway. "As it turns out," he disclosed, "those silly love songs are right. You're nobody 'til somebody loves you!" He paused for some time and then added, "I need somebody to love. And to love me back."

He inhaled deeply and loudly. The sound awakened the kitty. He caressed her again even though her cravings had been fed and she had stopped begging and gesturing for his touch. Manila Kitty purred in appreciation—feeble though it was.

As if to solidify his newfound commitment, in his aristocratic Texas gentleman's accent, he drawled, "If I ever get another chance up at bat, I'm going to change the way I play the game. No striking out this time, and no senseless swings at curve balls, either." Looking at the kitty, he remarked, "It's no longer an issue of the *quantity* of time that's at stake for me; it's about the *quality* of time now."

Sometime during the early morning hours, again Manila Kitty stirred and with a new urgency began to meow, awakening the sleeping giant. Automatically his hand reached to the kitten to offer his protection in the night.

This time the kitten could not be reassured. The man rolled over and turned on the light. Turning back to the kitten, he knew something was amiss. Gently touching her under the chin, he drew her head up to him and looked into her tiny face. The helplessness he saw there permeated his whole being. As though he could dissipate the pain he thought she must be feeling, he said tenderly, "You'll be all right, kitty. You'll be all right." Manila Kitty blinked her eyes slowly and meowed softly.

He thought she might be dying.

His eyes flooded with tears, and he began to grieve deeply. He placed both large hands upon the once demanding but no longer so feisty little creature and caressed her tenderly. But his grief went beyond the plight of the kitty. He shed tears over the transgression against his children— for not holding and hugging and helping them in all the ways they needed him to. The next stream of tears was about the negligence he felt toward the women he'd loved, but hadn't loved enough. These tears were followed by yet others for the many times he'd chosen to look the other way at "slight" injustices, rather than to help put an end to them. But the flood was yet to come: When the ledger of his transgressions was finally tallied, he closed his eyes and asked for forgiveness.

Like a rainbow holding promise to embark anew, a great sense of peace followed. And in that same moment, two destinies were consummated. Now with love filled, perhaps repaid, Manila Kitty was free. Her last days sweet, with a look of serene contentment on her face—as though her guardian angel had at last been pleased and appeased —Manila Kitty drew in her last breath and sweetly let it go.

And for the American from Texas, though their encounter had been brief, it was long enough to open his heart so he could confront his own mortality. And pledge to redefine *home*—a home where all love owed would be paid in full.

14 For Generals Only

"There are generals, admirals, captains and lieutenants. This class is for generals only! Generals!" the dapperly dressed man repeated firmly. "Those willing to think deeply and be decisive about what they've come to do— climb the mountain!"

All the faces were solemn—not that it concerned Dr. Laurent, my professor for the graduate-level management course I was taking. Pacing before the class and striking one hand with the pencil he held in the other, the three-star general continued to expound with didactic zeal on the need for aggression and determination on the battlegrounds of leadership. "Leadership is *not* for everyone," he said. "Only the finest, the strongest, the most determined *generals* will find themselves with a passing grade in this class!" he promised.

I found the course stimulating and challenging—especially with respect to earning high marks from Dr. Laurent. I was carrying a 4.0 grade-point average in my master's program, and expected to earn an A in this course, too—though to date, my overall grade in his class averaged a low B. With just two weeks to go until the course was over, the professor issued the last assignment, one that would account for a hefty 50 percent of the overall course grade.

Determined to get an A, I put in a great deal of effort on making sure that my paper was perfect. I confidently handed in my doctoral-level, award-winning work, absolutely convinced my professor would be as thoroughly impressed with it as I was!

On the day of our last class, Dr. Laurent handed back the graded papers, distributing each one individually on the appropriate student's desk as he walked up and down the aisles. Mine was one of the last to be returned. Rather than place it on my desk in front of me, the professor awkwardly slid the assignment under my arm from behind, almost as if to hide it. He then walked quickly to the front of the room and, within moments, dismissed the class.

I understood this odd presentation when I looked and saw, without any explanation or comment, the red letter "C" on the top right-hand corner of the cover page of my paper. Dumbfounded and embarrassed, I collected my things and left the classroom without a word. Feelings of failure, discouragement and injustice flooded my mind during the entire drive home. And the week that followed. So I went to speak with the professor.

Looking up from the paperwork in which he was absorbed, Dr. Laurent put down his pen. "I'm not surprised to see you here," he said kindly, his voice completely void of the military tone he employed in his classroom. "Actually, I've been expecting you. I suspect you've come to ask me about your grade, and tell me how unfair I've been."

"My sentiments, exactly," I replied stoically.

"Please allow me to explain," he said. "If you think I've treated you unfairly, then I've done my job to better prepare you for what you'll encounter as you climb the ranks, as you invariably will." At my stony silence, he added, "That's a compliment. But, you're a *general*. If you aspire to be a general, then *act* like one!"

"Just exactly what do you mean? My work in this class was excellent," I reasoned. "I followed your requests to the letter. What else should I have done?"

"Ships in a harbor are safe, but that's not what ships are meant for," he responded cryptically, then asked, "Did you agree with all I required you to do?"

"Well, no," I responded.

"Explain yourself," he instructed in a fatherly tone.

"Well," I said, wondering if disagreeing with him was a breach of protocol. "I thought the assignment on James was limiting."

"How so?" he asked, his direct gaze prompting me to candor.

"Well, you asked us to examine James in relation to his

theory of *ability*, but in the absence of *motivation*. The most important feature of James's work was that he proved beyond a shadow of a doubt that an extremely important function of leadership is motivation, and that employees generally work at about 30 percent of their *ability*, but close to 85 percent of their ability if highly *motivated*. If leaders are negligent in motivating people, then the performance of employees will suffer as much as if their ability were low."

"Why didn't you ask me if you could alter the assignment to include this faction?" Dr. Laurent questioned. Before I could defend myself, he asked, "And the second assignment?"

"I found the assignment on Taylor—the time and motion studies—well, pointless."

"And what would you have preferred to do instead?" he queried.

"The investigation by Mayo and the efficiency experts at the Western Electric Company was one of the most exciting and important ever undertaken in the field of motivational research," I explained, "most especially since it spawned the human relations movement. Mayo's findings paved the way for the work of McGregor, Herzberg, Hersey and Blanchard."

With these words the professor laughed good-naturedly and asked, "If you felt a different direction was needed, why didn't you come to me?"

"Because you said that the class was for generals, those who climb the mountain, so to speak," I replied in my own defense. "I didn't think you were open to being questioned."

"And so you didn't," he surmised. Then he asked me,

"Do you *really* think that just because you see a mountain you need to climb it? Is 'just because it's there' a good enough reason to venture up it?" His gaze pointed, he informed me, "*You needn't climb a mountain just because it's in your path.*" His meaningful expression and measured silence indicated I should absorb the phrase. "What if you wanted a *different* mountain to climb? In fact, what if you wanted to climb a mountain as something other than a general—say as a lieutenant or a queen? And, do you *really* think you need not question those in positions of authority? Do you see what I'm getting at? You need to find what you stand for. You need to find your own voice, examine it, discipline it and then *offer* it." Meeting my eyes, he continued, "I gave you a low grade because I was hoping to send a message that forced you to confront this matter. Otherwise, you'll just be one of the soldiers, like you have been throughout the course in tackling your assignments with grit and determination. Remember: Leadership is as much about *questioning* as it is about *doing*. What will *you* do in the face of having to consider the bottom line regardless of the cost to others? Will you sacrifice long-term goals for immediate results; or sacrifice truth in the name of expedience or convenience? Will *you* speak up, or not?"

Dr. Laurent paused to let the impact of his words sink in, and then said, "If I teach a student that she merely has to work hard to get a passing grade, she never learns the full meaning of climbing the mountain, never finds her own voice. Then it is *I* who have failed my generals." Now smiling, he added, "I'm really happy you're here. It tells me I was right about you." With that Dr. Laurent opened a drawer and withdrew a typed letter. He dated it by pen and handed it to me. The personalized letter, addressed to the department of records requested that my grade of C be removed and replaced with an A.

In a very real way Dr. Laurent's words and work are still working through the lives of his students and their students—like effective parenting lives on in our children's children. My professor was a sure and secure leader, one who wanted me to question which mountains were worth *my* climbing.

Over the years I've learned that generals come in all sizes and shapes. Sometimes we call them mentors, parents, friends or good teachers; sometimes thorns in our sides. Regardless of their titles, their steadfastness to worthy values and ideals inspires us to recalibrate our own, to want more from ourselves than what others may expect of us. And, their belief in us grants us the courage to transcend the safe harbor of doing something simply because we can.

Such exemplary and passionate leadership can teach us to question not only what we are doing but why, an act that causes us to move closer to discovering the real meaning and purpose of our lives. As Sir Edmund Hillary said, "It's not just the mountain we conquer but ourselves."

It is at such a time when each of us becomes a general.

15 Shoulder to Shoulder

At 5:00 A.M., driving along the coastal highway out of the small village of Del Mar that I call home, I noticed the mass of lights that filled the hillside, signaling the growing population of our tiny seaside town. As I looked at the houses, I recalled with nostalgia less crowded days and couldn't help thinking what a shame it was that we were losing what was once a cozy little beach community to ever-expanding population. Ironically, I was on my way to help build a house. I'd been invited by Linda Caldwell Fuller, cofounder of Habitat for Humanity, to participate in a "blitz build"—the building of a home in just one week—

in Southern California's Coachella Valley. And, the house we would build would be the model for the "First Ladies" house for Habitat for Humanity's Jimmy Carter Work Week the following spring in the Appalachian Mountains. This project, in turn, would serve as the kickoff project for some fifty houses to be built that week, and some ten thousand plus throughout the year.

"Welcome, Bettie!" Linda, a tall, sturdy, feminine woman, called to me when I got out of the car an hour and a half later. "You're just in time for breakfast. Come join me. I'll introduce you to the crew leaders and volunteers."

As we walked in the direction of the morning breakfast site, I looked at the parched land and was surprised that it was in such scruffy condition. "Is *this* it?" I asked, looking at the weed-ridden piece of dirt.

Her friendly sky blue eyes sparkling, and a warm and generous smile stretching from ear to ear, Linda replied enthusiastically, "Sure is!" Obviously seeing the soil as much more than land, she fervently confirmed, "*This* is the designated site!" With these words she stopped, put her hands on her hips and glanced around the patch of earth, the smile on her eyes and mouth lingering. "It's a *perfect* place for a home," she sighed. "A *Habitat* home."

Habitat for Humanity (which she cofounded with her husband, Millard Fuller) is a Christian, nonprofit housing ministry organized around the purpose of building and rehabilitating homes for families in need of, in Linda's own words, "decent housing." Habitat offers capital, not charity, so the "Habitat family" has to have sufficient income to meet the monthly payments. Those who qualify and are selected are also expected to participate both in building their own homes and those of other prospective home-owners, when possible. No profit and no interest are figured into the cost of the homes, making them affordable for low-income families. Habitat for Humanity is international in scope. To date, some 75,000 homes have been built around the globe. (Two of Habitat's most famous volunteers are former President Jimmy Carter and former First Lady Rosalynn Carter.)

Perhaps because of the early-morning hour, my imagination needed fueling. It was difficult for me to imagine that on this very spot a house would be built in just five days. I walked over to the wall map nearby and looked at an architect's rendering of the finished project. It showed a lovely one-story home complete with grass in the yard, several small trees in the backyard, small shrubs around the sides of the house and a sidewalk lined with bright pink flowers. It was a very serene and pretty picture.

Linda joined me in looking at the drawing. As she studied the rendering, a look of genuine contentment washed across this unpretentious and practical woman's face. "Amazing, isn't it," she remarked sweetly. "Whenever I see the new drawings of one of our homes for a Habitat family, I get the most incredible feeling inside. Of all the things I do, this is the most rewarding." The fullness of that satisfaction shone in her face as she added, "What can be more basic than to help another person build a *nest*—a home, a refuge, a place to be with family and friends?"

I considered it a rather interesting analogy. In just one week, where once there was just barren land, there would be a home. In his book, *Homing in the Presence*, Gerhard Frost says,

> *Observe the traffic of children if you would know the meaning of home. In every mood they turn toward home. Whatever their need of the moment, they are great homers. Sometimes with a tear on each cheek; sometimes with a secret too good to keep; sometimes with a question that won't wait, sometimes just hungry, or tired or guilty—always we turn toward home —a symbol of acceptance, safety and love.*[1]

"A *nest*," I teased. "I find that a really loving metaphor."
"A nest with five little *souls* inside," she said smiling.

After breakfast and an orientation of how the week would unfold, the crew leader handed me, along with forty other volunteers assembled from around the country— skilled and unskilled, young and old—a tool belt, hard hat and list of assigned duties for each of the five days. "One, two, three, blitz!" the crew leader called, signaling it was time to begin.

Blitzing is an interesting process. The week prior to the forty volunteers assembling for the building of the home, the slab is poured and trusses are built by local community volunteers. And then the "blitz" moves in and begins work at a staggering pace. Wall panels and roof trusses go up the first day. On day two, drywall and interior framing begin. On day three, the roof is sheeted with plywood, and

---

[1] Gerhard Frost, *Homing in the Presence: Meditations for Daily Living* (New York: Harper & Row, 1978), 116.

windows and doors go on. The primary focus of day four is insulation and stucco, and on the fifth day it's plumbing fixtures, cabinets, interior doors, garage doors, tile on the roof, air conditioning unit, carpets, floor covering and hardware. In addition to that, all interior and exterior painting is completed, drapes are installed, and, finally, the lawn is planted. At the end of a five-day "blitz," from an empty lot a house "sprouts," and a family moves in to make it a home.

The nest we were building was for the Marez family, who had lost their home through a series of catastrophic events. They are a family of five: Ray Marez, a maintenance worker for Morningside Homeowners Association and sole provider for the family; his wife, Ronda, a former bookkeeper who suffered an aneurysm that paralyzed her left side, leaving her disabled and unemployable; and their three children: Rachel, Matthew and Michael. Their new home would accommodate Ronda's disability.

Each day volunteers from different states across the nation and with diverse backgrounds and professions diligently worked to build the house. Janet Loren from Palm Desert and Sandra Graham, area director for three regions covering six southeastern states, were the key organizers for this build. Cathy Belatti was there with her daughter, Alyson—who within the same year had blitzed homes for Habitat in Africa and Mexico. Ruthann Kallenberg, from Georgia, had just returned from a Global Village work camp in Fiji; Donna Guthrie celebrated her fiftieth birthday by pledging to walk five miles in all fifty states to raise money for Habitat (she had only two states to go). Support came from everywhere: Debra Goodwin, an

American Airlines pilot, from Fort Worth, Texas; Mary Beth
Irvine from Boring, Oregon; Judy Crabil from Arizona;
neighboring churches and the local women's clubs who
prepared and served lunch and dinner, and opened their
homes to host get-togethers for the crew; as well as the
hotel proprietors who provided rooms at reduced rates.

Watching everyone work and observing how the community rallied to support the work going on reminded me
of the soothing and powerful words of my mother, who,
less than a month ago when I complained of the difficult
and demanding schedule ahead of me, had counseled,
"We're here for you. Know that your family is not just
behind you, but rather standing with you, shoulder to
shoulder—all the way." For me, these words of connection,
caring and support were an anchor offering untold
strength. Perhaps the Marez family felt that same strength
as an entire crew of workers stood side by side—shoulder
to shoulder—helping them build their "nest."

Late afternoon of the fifth day, the house was complete,
looking every bit like the rendering! Tears of joy and gratitude were everywhere. I spotted Linda busy preparing for
the upcoming dedication. With this loving woman's leadership, "dirt" had been transformed into a "decent" house.
The Marez family, once in need of a decent house, stood
looking at their new property, one that had been no more
than an empty lot, a roll of blueprints and a dream just a
week before. The littlest boy summed it up best. "Wow!" he
exclaimed, "a house with a *yard!*"

Her eyes misty, Linda now dedicated the home. "Mr.
and Mrs. Marez, it's my honor," she paused, catching my

eyes, "as we all stand shoulder to shoulder with you, to present you with the keys to your new home." As is her custom, Linda, sincere, with humor as her second nature, a woman who amasses goodwill wherever she goes, held a Bible out for them with the keys to their new house placed on top of it.

This is as it should be: standing together, not merely behind each other. We must stand shoulder to shoulder, where we find that the bonds of humanity can supersede the distance of miles, age, gender, color and creed. And to help each other when in need, to build a *nest*—a home, a refuge, a place to be with family and friends.

Like the others, I left with blisters on my hands and a few aches, too. But I also took with me an astonishing discovery. As I drove home along the darkened highway and into the small town of Del Mar that night, I once again noticed the hillside filled with lights. But on this night, I saw something very different from an overpopulation of houses—an assessment I had made just five days previously in the early morning hours. Now before me lay a vast galaxy of twinkling lights nestled into the beautiful hillside near the ocean. And the sight was pleasing, satisfying, full.

This shift in perspective was so dramatic that I pulled over to the side of the road to spend a few moments observing the lights. It was then that the sea breeze carried Linda's poignant words back to me: "What can be more basic than to help another person build a nest—a home, a refuge, a place to be with family and friends?" With that thought came the realization that these lights were more than houses: *Souls* rested in these nests. With this shift in perspective, the splendor of the hillside of twinkling lights was even more resplendent.

Sometimes, it's simply a space inside our hearts that grants us a stunning new perspective. Often, it's in the act of working shoulder to shoulder to help another soul in the world through which we are able to discover that sacred space inside our own heart.

As planned, the following June I joined Linda and Habitat for Humanity International as we gathered again to blitz a home, this time for Pam Sykes and her son Jordan in Pikeville, Kentucky, in the Appalachian Mountains. Standing shoulder to shoulder to build the nest were First Lady Hillary Rodham Clinton, former First Lady Rosalynn Carter, First Lady of Oklahoma Cathy Keaton, First Lady of Kentucky Judi Patton, former First Lady of Virginia Jinx Holton, Washington attorney Holly Eaton, and many other volunteers—all of whom set aside political, career and personal differences to stand shoulder to shoulder to help another soul build a *nest*—a home, a refuge, a place to be with family and friends.

As with the other builders, throughout the week I marveled at the work going on. Ladders stood, paint cans perched on the unfolded shelves near their top rungs, as paint-spattered women leaned from lower rungs, rolling color on the walls. Other workers buzzed about, wearing tool belts and hard hats, lugging plumbing parts or sheets of drywall, all engaged in their assigned tasks with focused intensity. The cacophony of hammers pounding and a welder's forceful flame-spewing roar filled the air. But in addition to the physical completion of the day-to-day work, I noticed that working together for such a common cause is an equalizer. It does not matter the high school or college from which each volunteer graduated, nor the rank, rating or prestige of that school. Professional titles and affiliations melt away. It does not matter what law firm or corporation you work for, or how well your latest book is selling. It does not matter whether you are a first lady of your state—or first lady of your company or household. It matters not your color, creed, country or political-party affiliation. Helping a family build a *nest*—a home, a refuge, a place to be with family and friends—transcends all lines.

The camaraderie and cooperation—the humanity—of working shoulder to shoulder with others serves as a reminder to us all that people working together with a common goal is a taste berry of unparalleled importance.

16 The Denver Connection

"Could you *please* tell me where I'm supposed to go?" the disheveled woman begged of no one in particular, waving her airline tickets in front of her. I was sitting in the Denver airport waiting for my connecting flight when she seemed to appear out of nowhere. Her brown hair was as untamed as her demeanor. It sprang out in odd wisps of uncombed or windblown tangles. Huffing and puffing, the flustered woman looked wildly about for *any* sort of assistance. When she spotted the gate attendant absently shuffling papers at her workstation, the woman headed straight for her. It was a good hour before check-in time for the next scheduled departure from this gate, so no people were in line yet.

Nearly at a full run, the lost woman practically tripped on my feet as she rounded the corner to reach the agent. Not that she would have noticed: the lenses of the black-rimmed glasses perched askew on the end of her nose were so smudged I'm surprised she could see through them at all. With her blouse only half-tucked into her wrinkled skirt, her clothes were in the same disarray as her hair and her emotions.

"Miss! Oh, Miss!" she called, trying frantically to alert the attendant as she plowed her way to the counter. Both her hands flailed around in search of something in the large oversized bag that swung from her shoulders. But it wasn't the sound of the woman's voice that elicited the attention of the gate attendant. Rather, it was the thud of her over-sized purse as it slipped from her shoulder and crashed to the floor. There it lay in a heap, its scattered contents madly rolling away in all directions. Now on her hands and knees, the woman grabbed for a silver-cased tube of lipstick rolling full speed ahead and then dove at another escaping in the opposite direction. As the woman lunged for this item, her glasses slid off her nose and fell to the floor, but not before her bulging clump of hair, restrained only by an old battered barrette, gave way and plopped over her brow and into her face.

"Are you on this flight?" the attendant asked coolly.

"Well, I don't know," the woman stammered. "I don't think so, but maybe. Where am I?"

Unfazed by the perplexed woman's chaotic "lost" look, the

attendant continued arranging the items on her counter in preparation for the next scheduled departure. Looking up only briefly, the attendant informed her, "You're at Gate C78."

Scooping up the last of the spilled contents from her purse, the woman got up. "Am I supposed to be here?" she implored, eyes casting about for some sort of mysterious visual clue.

"I don't know, are you?" the attendant replied, this time without looking up.

"Well, I have to be somewhere because when I went to the other gate, they told me the plane had already took off!" the woman explained, hoisting the purse back upon her shoulder and readjusting its long shoulder straps. Looking genuinely baffled, she laid her tickets on the agent's counter. "So, what should I do?" she asked woefully.

The attendant leaned over the counter. Without picking the tickets up, she spared them a cursory glance. "You're supposed to be at Gate *B*78," she placidly explained. "Raleigh, North Carolina, leaves from the B concourse."

"My sister lives in *South* Carolina," the woman retorted. "I'm going to South Carolina to visit her."

"Then you are not only in the wrong terminal," the attendant pointed out, "but headed for the wrong state. Your ticket reads Raleigh, *North* Carolina."

"Are you sure?" the woman asked, retrieving her tickets from the gate attendant. As though her ticket were hiding information from her, she studied it closer, trying to decipher what the words and numbers on it *really* meant. "How could this be?" she asked. "I have to get where I'm going!"

"Ma'am, if you don't know where you're supposed to be," the attendant directed calmly, "I suggest you return to the customer service center where I'm sure they can help you."

"The *service center*," the woman repeated vacantly. "Where's that? How do I get there?"

"It's in the main lobby. Just turn left, follow the signs," the attendant instructed professionally.

Flustered, the woman lamented, "But won't I miss my flight if I have to go all the way there?"

"I'm certain they'll be able to help you," the attendant reiterated in a dry monotone. Deliberately looking away from the woman she then summarily turned her attention to the three smartly dressed businesspeople who had just arrived. All three watched in silent disbelief, trying as best they could to politely stifle their ear-to-ear smirks. A mannerly smile came to life on the attendant's face. "How can I help you?" she asked them with sweet solicitude, ignoring the woman who stood to the side of the counter still thoroughly lost.

The attendant slowly took the tickets of the business travelers with all the graciousness of a good hostess and left the woman standing there in confusion. One of the business travelers now being assisted by the attendant whispered something to the attendant, and the two of them broke out in restrained laughter.

While most onlookers rolled their eyes in sympathetic yet amused recognition of the woman's comedy of errors, it was one of those scenes that wasn't all that funny. Obviously new to the airport environment, and having already missed an earlier flight on her own account, the visibly frazzled woman had no idea what to do next.

I could definitely relate. "Traveling is not for the faint of heart," Art Linkletter is quoted as saying. He's right. Sometimes (experienced or not) traveling can be trying.

Several years ago while in Japan on business, I decided to take the bullet train to Kyoto to observe the festive and traditional "Old World" style of bringing in the New Year. As I stood in the train station buying a ticket, I soon learned that the ticket agent didn't speak English.

I didn't speak Japanese. Pointing to my "Temples of Kyoto" brochure, I announced, "Kyoto." The man behind the counter smiled, took an assortment of yen from my hand, returned fewer bills of an even stranger denomination, smiled again, and pointed me to the left.

Merrily I walked left, only to discover dozens upon dozens of signs overhead, all urgently flashing in one of four colors. They obviously announced the arriving and departing trains, but from where to where I had no clue. Everything was in Japanese—foreign symbols to me.

If truth be known, I asked no fewer than five people for help in steering me in the direction of the appropriate train to Kyoto. Pointing to my ticket, I said, "Kyoto?" to the unoccupied business traveler with a ticket in his hand. He looked at me, smiled coyly, and pointed left. After several minutes of walking left, I realized that while hundreds of people were coming toward me, I was the only one going in the opposite direction. Once again I pointed to my ticket and asked a traveler, "Kyoto?" This time, the person pointed to the right. As did the third. Two who agreed: Obviously I needed to go right.

So I did. I soon found myself in an area of the train station in which only schoolchildren were boarding trains. "Kyoto?" I asked the studious-looking young boy with a backpack.

"Oh, no, no," he said, pointing to the tracks in this section of the station. Then, pointing to the left, he uttered an unequivocal "Kyoto."

Five minutes into "left" put me right back where I started. So of course, I asked yet again. When the fifth respondent pointed left, I was baffled. I stood for a moment considering what to do next. Luckily for me, in that same moment a train arrived. The door opened and the conductor stepped to the door shouting, "Kyoto, Kyoto." He said other things, too, none of which I understood.

While I know of at least two other regions in the world named Kyoto, on this night I was sure this train was headed to the Kyoto I was determined to see! Luckily for me, it turned out to be the right train, and it was one of the most gloriously adventurous holidays I've had! Still, in getting on the right train, I had been no less baffled than the woman who didn't know how to get around in an airport. She had missed her flight because she had erroneously been steered to gate C78 instead of B78, the gate from which her flight had now departed—though it wasn't really the correct gate after all, because she wanted to go to South Carolina rather than North Carolina. Perhaps the departures and arrivals monitors in the Denver airport looked as foreign to her as the Arrivals and Departures monitors in the Japanese train station did to me. The woman hustled recklessly from one gate to the next. She asked whoever she came upon for direction. Her only other compass was her frantic fogged interpretation of these varied, passing instructions—mine had been much the same in the train station.

Now the woman stood in a totally different wing of the airport. She was drastically off course from where she needed to be and was confused and befuddled. "So what should I do *now*?" she wailed to no one in particular.

Without hesitating, a businesswoman stood up, quickly smoothing any wrinkles from the skirt of her chic two-piece business suit. She approached the lost woman and asked lovingly, "Where is it you need to get to, dear?"

Wiping the tears welling in her eyes with a hand that shook, the bewildered traveler sniffled, momentarily unable to speak.

"Here, let me see your tickets," the helpful businesswoman coaxed, taking the tickets from the hand of the sister of a woman who lived in South Carolina. She then placed an arm around the lost woman and pointed out the monitors above the different counters. Looking from the tickets to the monitors, the businesswoman efficiently explained how to read the monitor to the weary traveler.

It was helpful information. With a look of sheer gratitude on her face, the woman asked, "And you say I can get there by going this way?"

The businesswoman in the wool suit looked at her watch. "I have a little time before my flight," she said. "I can take you there if you like."

"Oh, thank you," the woman said earnestly. "It's my first time in an airport. I usually take the bus to visit my sister, but it's such a long way."

"I know the feeling," the businesswoman said. "The first time I was in an airport I was rather uncertain myself."

The woman, now soothed, was eager to talk. "Oh, I know what you mean," she said. "Last week when I took the bus to visit a dear friend across town, a young boy sitting across from me was whimpering. When I asked him why he was crying, he said it was because he was frightened that he wouldn't know when to get off at the correct stop. See, he didn't know that the driver called out the stops and that's one way to know when it's time to get off the bus. But when I told him how it was done, he sat up straight and paid attention to every stop the driver called out. I could tell he was really relieved."

To paraphrase the song, we all need a little help from our friends.

17

One, One, One . . .

"I have lived like an animal in the street," the dying man whispered, "but I am going to die as an angel, loved and cared for." These words found a home in the enormous heart of the tiny woman bent over the emaciated man. Her hands delicately removed the worms from the wounds of his body. The genuine gratitude and heartfelt thanks expressed in the eyes of this suffering man touched her, but she didn't need to be thanked: The benevolent love, acceptance and compassion that shone in her eyes and the warmth of her generous smile were intended to nourish *his* spirit.

Mustering the strength to speak, he asked, "Who *is* this *angel* caring for me?"

"Your sister," she replied.

"Sister," he said with a peaceful smile on his face, "I'm going home to God now." Exhaling his last breath, the man died.

Who was this "angel"? She was Agnes Gonxha Bojaxhiu, born August 26, 1910, in Yugoslavia, better known to the world as Mother Teresa. On September 6, 1997, she left this world, but she left it a better place. After the night Mother Teresa picked up one dying man from a sewer in Calcutta, providing love and comfort while he passed over, she and the sisters in her Missionaries of Charity picked up more than 40,000 dying people—many of whom, because of their caretaking, survived.

In the spring of 1997, I was so inspired by this remarkable woman's life and work, especially after hearing this poignant story, that I sent her the manuscript of a book I was writing in hopes that she might provide an endorsement. I didn't really think I'd get a reply from the tiny, eighty-seven-year-old world citizen, a frail woman who was busy meeting with powerful kings and queens and popes and priests—and hundreds of the sick and dying.

But I did.

Mother Teresa not only read my manuscript, she called me! "You must stop walking in the middle of the road!" she rebuked. "You must be more willing to write what you *know!*" She was referring to my spiritual beliefs. I am a Christian, though she feels that in my writing I'm not pressing hard enough to reveal that identity. Using a well-known cliché of hers, she chided, "You, me, all of us—we are but a pencil in the hand of God. All of us, no matter what our station in life, no matter how easy or difficult our lives may seem, we are all called to be a pencil in the hand of God. You must write the words, each one, written as one who writes for God."

I can hardly believe I challenged her, but I did. "But Mother Teresa," I informed her, "I believe my mission is not to lead people to God, but rather to their hearts. I want my work to inspire others to see life from the eyes of their hearts. Hopefully, that's where they'll find God."

"Mainstream is not the point," she exhorted. "If even one reader is touched by you alone—because the truth is clearly written—then you will have done God's will. *Your* will is quite beside the point."

"But that's your gift. I . . ."

"Nonsense," she retorted. "I do not think I have any special qualities, I don't claim anything for the work. It is his work. I am like a little pencil in his hand, that is all. He does the thinking. He does the writing. The pencil has nothing to do with it. The pencil has only to be allowed to be used."

If God is the hand that writes, we each are the instrument. Mother Teresa wanted me, wanted all of us, to understand that the message is delivered in the way we live our lives and the way we express ourselves in our lives and through our work. What we do in our lives affects our hearts and alters our souls. Our behavior changes the "condition" of our souls. "You must put away your excuses," she told me bluntly. "Your words soothe suffering and create happiness. They must also further an understanding of God."

Just as she expected me to "put away my excuses," she expected us all to help our fellow man. And she believed with all her might that we will—as Prince Michael of Greece quickly discovered in an interview with her. He told her, "There may be hope in the streets of India, but there is little or none in the streets here."

"Oh, no!" she burst out defiantly. "That can't be! There are many people ready to help."

What can we learn from this tiny, humble—and feisty— woman whose voice reduced a massive planet to the size of an oyster? First, there are no mediocre souls. In this she acknowledged, "All are worthy to be served." With this reminder, she quickly pointed out that it is not just the sick or impoverished who are in need of our service. She said, "Being unwanted, unloved, uncared for is the *greatest* poverty in the world."

Second, we learn that perspective is an important dimension. "I never look at the masses as my responsibility," she said. "I look at the *individual*. I can love only one person at a time. I can feed only one person at a time. Just one, one, one. So I begin. I pick up one person, one, one, one. . . ."

"One, one, one" has enormous connotations. Consider for a moment the far-reaching implication of the word "locally" in the axiom "Think globally, act locally." As my friend, the author Dr. Denis Waitley, wrote in an endorsement for my book *Values from the Heartland*, "World peace is learned at the knee of a parent, or someone acting in that behalf." At the very heart of "one, one, one" is the significance and importance of our day-to-day actions—all of them—in both words and deeds. Our actions with our children, families, coworkers, students, patients—even those with whom we come into contact only briefly—touch and affect lives more profoundly than we know. In my case, Mother Teresa's admonition caused me to think deeply about my work and the words I use to express it. Her sentiment is ever present in my mind, her influence slowly but surely taking hold within.

I am reminded of the story of the man jogging on the beach who came across a young boy picking up starfish, frantically slinging them into the ocean. "I'm afraid your efforts are in vain, young man!" the jogger said as he approached the boy. "Hundreds of starfish have been washed ashore here, and they're withering fast in the hot sun. Your well-intentioned efforts simply aren't going to make a difference. You might as well run along and play." The boy surveyed the many starfish stranded on the beach, then looked at the beautiful starfish he was holding. Flinging it into the ocean, he replied optimistically, "Well, I made a difference to that one!"

This little story illuminates an ideal Mother Teresa wanted us to take to heart: We must never underestimate how crucial our actions are. Just as the boy's singular actions made a difference to each individual starfish he touched, just as Mother Teresa and the Missionaries of Charity made a difference to each person they cared for, we each make a difference when we reach out to each other—helping, supporting, assisting—one, one, one.

"What is the single most important thing we can do to make the world a better place?" a reporter once asked Mother Teresa. Again she gifted us with insight that could well serve as the basis for a lifelong homework assignment. She simply said, "We must find each other."

"How do we find each other?" he asked.

"We find each other, one by one by one," she answered. "Maybe if I didn't pick up that one person I wouldn't have picked up 42,000," she said, encouraging us to begin with just one fellow human being, one single act of kindness. "The whole work is only a drop in the ocean. But if I didn't put the drop in, the ocean would be one drop less."

Mother Teresa—one of the great taste berries of our times—counseled, "Same thing for you, same thing in your family, same thing in your community and everywhere you go. Just begin . . . one, one, one."

18

The Gift of Subira

She lay in a classic feline pose, legs stretched out, head proudly held high, turned to one side, a classic pose that delights high-fashion photographers—and the many who came to have their picture taken with her. No stranger to celebrity, her perfect features graced cards, stationery, newsletters; her strong and supple body played centerfold to many a lovely frame on bed stands, dresser tops and mahogany desks. Gorgeous, regal and, though young, she was principal ambassador to the kingdom of Shambala and known throughout the world as a wondrous symbol of beauty and raw energy, and circumstantial luck.

"Subira is her name," the lovely woman, clad in jeans, boots and buckskin coat, said, beaming. Thoughtfully, she looked at the small group of young people who were there on a field trip from a local rehab center. With gentle affection in her voice, the woman said, "She's a three-year-old cheetah, not even at the height of her game. Magnificent, isn't she!"

As though it were a well-rehearsed script, Subira turned her head to the audience and gazed into the crowd. Her eyes, with their horseshoe black lines angling back from their corners and running to her mouth, looked as though they were freshly painted on for the day's exhibition. So dazzling was her rich coat of closely set black spots on a tawny-colored backdrop of thick fur that all felt compelled to comment, "Oooooh, look at her. She's so beautiful!" With a look that was both content and alert, as though she knew they found her captivating, Subira cocked her royal head and, with a serene gaze, assessed her many admirers.

All continued to stare in awe—except for a teenage boy in the back row, who groaned in what seemed boredom and discontent. When several members of the group turned in his direction, in a macho-posture-to-impress he rolled up the sleeves of his white shirt, further exposing his well-developed muscles. To no one in particular he barked, "What are you looking at?"

The woman paid no attention. "The cheetah is the fastest land animal on earth," she told the small crowd. "Aren't you, honey?" she asked in a playful velvety tone, looking over her shoulder at the exquisite animal that lay atop the large, long, low branch of a massive oak tree.

Once again facing the group of young people who had come to observe the beauty of this spectacular animal and the other wild cats in this unique sanctuary, the woman continued characterizing the animal. "Cheetahs are able to achieve speeds of seventy miles per hour for short durations. They hunt in short spurts that are like the sprints of a track star. And from a standstill, the cheetah can accelerate to forty-five miles per hour in just two seconds, with bounds that measure twenty-five feet. Just imagine! In the wild, the cheetah races after its prey, unlike most cats, which usually pounce on their victims. She uses her heavy tail for balance when executing sharp turns." Though she'd recited the facts of the cheetah many times to visiting crowds, her obvious enthusiasm and excitement shone in her face.

"Do they eat humans?" a teen in the crowd inquired.

"To the best of my knowledge, no human has ever been killed by a cheetah," the woman thoughtfully replied. She continued, "As you can see, Subira's head and body are about five feet long, with a two-and-a-half-foot tail. She stands about thirty-nine inches at the shoulder thanks to her long, slender legs. Her weight will max out around 140 pounds." Suddenly, almost as if on cue, Subira got to her feet and leapt from her perch. Once on the ground, she began gracefully walking around inside the large enclosure that contained her. The group fell silent at the awesome sight of this beautiful beast in motion.

A knowing smile swept across the woman's face as she anticipated what was to come, and what happened every time people first encounter Subira. It was just a matter of when.

I was sitting in the front row of chairs assembled for the group. "They haven't noticed . . . yet," the woman, a friend of mine, mouthed to me. Her winsome blue eyes gave the impression of a child who had a wonderful secret and could barely contain it. She continued, "It's not easy in the wild to run down animals that are also speedy. That's because cheetahs can only run at high speeds for short distances. A strong antelope, for instance, can often weave or zig-zag enough to escape a cheetah's pursuit. So sometimes a hungry cheetah has to wait several days to find a meal."

Impressed by the beauty and grace of the animal, and revealing that she understood the cheetah is an animal facing extinction, the young dark-haired girl in the front row asked, "I'm sorry, I don't know your name, but I have a question. Is that why they're endangered?"

"Oh, I'm sorry, I forgot to introduce myself," the woman responded. "My name is Tippi. Tippi Hedren. You can call me Tippi. And to answer your question, the two main reasons cheetahs are endangered are poachers and loss of habitat. Poachers illegally hunt and kill cheetahs for their fur, which they sell on the black market. The loss of habitat has occurred over time as man continually encroaches on their environment."

The group momentarily fell silent. With an engaging half-cocked smile, Tippi looked first to the cheetah and then to the crowd and then back to the cheetah, then walked over and sat close to the fence that contained the animal. It was easy to see that Subira was smitten with his mistress. The exquisite animal hummed wondrously and purred persuasively. The love affair was mutual.

"Ohhhhh," Tippi cooed, "what glorious sounds from your magnificent throat."

Tippi Hedren is no stranger to early morning sounds of the wild. Every dawn, as faint traces of pink begin to color the sky over her home nestled in the awesome grandeur of California's Soledad Canyon, the big cats roar, their deep-bellied choruses rumbling in sequence, some overlapping. She calls her home *Shambala*—Sanskrit for "a meeting place of peace and harmony for all beings, animal and human." Shambala is tucked into the Santa Clara Valley, forty miles north of Los Angeles. With the Angeles National Forest and San Gabriel Range nearby, Shambala spreads along the narrow Santa Clara River for about a quarter mile. It resembles parts of the African riverine woodland, though the trees are mainly tall cottonwoods instead of the savanna's thorny acacias. Replicating the raw beauty of the *kopjes* of the Serengeti and Manyara, gigantic brown rock outcroppings lay randomly dispersed throughout the sprawling land. It is, quite simply, breath-taking. Here, in an environment so like their native home, the lions roar in unison until that final strange bark from the dominant lead cat that says the conversation is over.

Abruptly, as though disgusted by all this affection, the boy in the back row mocked, "Big deal. A big, skinny cat with a bunch of spots that runs fast. So what! Next! Bring out the stupid tigers or whatever so we can get this over with!" Embarrassed by the rude outburst, the other members of the group turned and looked at the boy in disapproval. Tippi also observed the adolescent but made no response to his comment.

But the cheetah did. Looking in the teenager's direction, the cheetah instantly began chirping.

Using this behavior as a cue for her next statement, Tippi informed the group, "Cheetahs have certain sounds that are unique to each animal alone—a voice print similar to that of individual humans. A happy sound is a distinct chirp, like the one you are hearing now. Her hungry sound is a throaty vibration, and her way of saying 'watch out' is her warning noise that sounds like a high two-pitched hum. But as you can hear by all this chirping, she's pretty happy. In fact, I think she likes you," she said, looking directly at the boy.

"Yeah, yeah, sure! She just loves me," the boy mimicked sarcastically. Again, Ms. Hedren continued without responding to his ill-mannered remark. She knew from experience that *something* had happened to make this boy so angry and full of spite.

Tippi's presentation to the group hadn't been planned. It's the job of her staff to share Shambala's history and educate those who come to visit. She and I had simply been passing by when the group assembled. With the staff member waiting, Tippi now turned it over to a young assistant. Turning to me, Tippi motioned that we continue on our way. As we did, we turned to observe the group. It was from that vantage point we saw the belligerent boy with the smart, quick mouth—an image that revealed something his words hadn't. Clad in a T-shirt, a fit torso emerged, one that sat tensely in a wheelchair. One empty pant leg, folded under, hung next to the remaining leg and tennis shoe.

Seventeen-year-old Cory had dreams of playing major league baseball one day. That was his one and only goal. He lived and breathed baseball and dreamed of the day when he would have a following, fans who knew he was "the man." No one doubted Cory's ability, certainly not Bob Shepard, the lead university scout for baseball talent in the state. He had recruited Cory, confirming a promising future. That was before the accident that had claimed his right leg. Nothing could replace the joy that the accident dashed.

Cory lost more than his leg in the tragic car accident: He also lost his hope. And his spirit. It left him not only physically disabled, but emotionally crippled. Unable to dream a goal that was anything other than being a major baseball talent, he was bitter, jaded and feeling just plain useless. Hopeless. He sat in a wheelchair with a chip on his shoulder, angry at the world and, today, on another "boring field trip" from the rehab program.

Unwilling and unable, Cory had become one of the rehab center's few "un" patients: unable to reconstruct a plan for his life, one that compensated for the loss of one leg and didn't allow excuses to impede it; unable to summon the courage to dream new plans for the future. He gave up on not only himself but others. "Get off my back," he had told the rehab director. "You can't help me. No one can."

Upon seeing the image of the boy and the missing leg, Tippi wanted to stay longer. As though she knew something was about to unfold, she turned to me and said, "This is usually the best part. Let's stay a while longer. Once that boy sees *this* he'll *never* forget it."

We stood close by as the new group's guide continued. "Cheetahs never feed on carrion. They eat fresh meat—though in captivity, they do like people food!"

The word was somehow of interest to the boy.

"Carrion?" the angry-at-the-world young man boisterously questioned, "What's that mean?"

"Cadaver, corpse, remains," the young assistant responded.

Cory smirked. "So the cheetah doesn't eat roadkill," he taunted loudly in response.

Upon hearing the boy's guttural sound, the glorious animal once again took up her efficacious purr. The audience, enchanted once again by Subira's glorious sound, cooed in hushed unison, "Ohhhhh!"

Enjoying their positive response—and always willing to flaunt—Subira decided to give them a show of her skills. As if to say, "I can please you more. Watch and let me show you how fast these spots can fly," Subira instantly began blazing a trail of speed around the enclosure encircling the awestruck spectators. "Ahhhhh," sighed the crowd, "she's so fast."

Then, it finally happened: They noticed! "She only has three legs!" the crowd gasped. "Oh, no!" the girl in the front row exclaimed, rising from her seat. The other astonished young people looked on in silence, aghast at what they saw.

No one was more stunned by the sight of this incredible animal running at full speed than Cory. Looking bewildered, he verbalized what the others were thinking. "How can she run that fast with three legs?" Amazed at the cheetah's effortless, seemingly natural movements, in a whisper, he remarked, "Incredible. Just incredible." And then, a miracle happened. Staring at the young strong beast with the missing leg, Cory smiled, a look of sheer amazement spreading across his face.

Seizing the moment of opportunity, Tippi walked back to face the young people, telling them, "As you have now all noticed, Subira is very special. She has refused to let what many deemed a gross defect get in her way, and she has adapted very successfully. Since no one told her she shouldn't—or couldn't—run as fast as a cheetah with four legs, she doesn't know otherwise. And, so, she can. In some respects her condition makes her more endearing, and yet she deserves the attention she gets. Because she has adapted she earns the respect from all of us; that provides her with yet more contact, and even more adulation. So in many ways, her missing leg sets up a condition where she gets more of everything, really." Tippi paused for a moment and, turning to Subira, continued by saying, "We just love her. She's a living example, a symbol, of what Shambala is all about . . . recognizing the value of all living things, even if, for whatever reason, they are different. And learning that at the height of our limitations, we find the strength of our love."

The boy now listened with interest as Tippi explained Subira's history. "Subira's umbilical cord was wrapped around her leg in the womb, so it atrophied, causing her to lose the leg soon after she was born. Born in an Oregon zoo, but with only three legs, she was cast off. Her fate seemed hopeless. They were considering euthanasia— putting her to sleep."

Surprised, Cory asked thoughtfully, "Why?"

"Because," Tippi responded, "they thought, 'What good is a three-legged cheetah? What would people say?' They didn't think the public would want to see a deformed cheetah. Since it was felt that she wouldn't be able to adapt, you know, to run and act like a normal cheetah, she served no purpose. She had nothing to do. But we all need to do *something*, don't we?" With a kind and wistful look, she looked into Cory's face. "That's when we heard about Subira and offered our sanctuary where she could live as normal a life as possible," Tippi said. "It was soon after she came to us that she demonstrated her own worth—a unique gift of love and spirit. As I mentioned earlier, normally cheetahs are solitary animals, but not this cheetah. She decided to love people, and made herself part of the family immediately. Subira has touched the lives of people around the world, and has become our most persuasive spokesman for promoting our message and cause. Though discarded because she was an imperfect animal in a world that demands perfection, she had to create her own worth by adapting to something new. We are so happy to have her. We need her. She truly is a most cherished and priceless gift."

Abandoning all wisecracks, Cory grew reflective. Inspired, he asked softly, "Can I touch her?"

Perhaps in that poignant moment the boy understood that Subira's courage did not allow a missing leg to hinder her—and that opened the gates of his own heart and mind. Whatever it was, it changed his demeanor and willingness to participate. When the leader of the visiting group was preparing to leave at the end of the tour and asked for a volunteer to push and hold the large rolling gate open so the van could exit the ranch, Cory dared to take his first step in creating his own worth. He volunteered.

As the rest of the group looked on, Cory wheeled himself over to the gate. Struggling to maneuver it open, he gripped the high-wire fence for support and pushed it open. The expression on his face as he continued to hold the gate until the van passed through was one of great determination and satisfaction. And, judging from the smile on his face, it appeared that Cory took his first step in opening to the possibility of victory over the challenges he faced.

I looked back at the beautiful sleek cat, now an observer from the large oak branch in her compound. There was a peaceful look of contentment on her face as she gracefully groomed herself. It was, for her, just another interesting day in the beautiful dwellings of Shambala where a certain magical element is present in the ongoing day-to-day happenstance, one she finds both stimulating and intriguing. It was just another demonstration—to yet another human—of creating self-worth, hope and purpose.

19   Horse Sense!

A man I once dated *loved* horses. I loved *him* more than I loved his love for horses!

One of his greatest desires was for me to share his love for horses and want to spend as much time with them as he did. To accomplish this, he took me riding as often as he could, believing that with enough practice (time *on* the horse), I would not only become a good rider but would fall in love with horses, too.

While riding in the Cuyamaca Mountains on one of these outings, we steered our horses off a cleared trail and into a densely wooded area. Several steps into the trees, my horse reared into the air. Alarmed that my horse was spooked, I yanked on the reins in an effort to control him. The horse reared again, and this time tried to throw me off, which he did. I thought that the horse was simply a mean-spirited, ill-mannered creature—one I wasn't about to get back on.

"Why'd he do that?" I yelled to Geoffrey.

"Just get back on," Geoffrey called to me nonchalantly, ignoring my question.

"Absolutely not," I cried. "I'm not about to get thrown off again."

"Well," he mocked, "after a couple more times on the ground, you'll decide not to fall off." Laughing, he added, "Or, you'll get good at falling!"

Geoffrey's approach to sharing his passion for riding was not working. His style reminded me of an experience I had as a young child learning to swim. The instructor, Mrs. Paulson, took our class of three children up to the highest diving board at the local pool. In one fell swoop, she pushed all of us off. Luckily we tumbled in different directions so that we didn't hit each other as we plunged ten feet into the pool—or drown each other as we struggled to the surface, gasping for air and sucking the chlorinated water into our lungs.

Mrs. Paulson's style of "sink or swim" was not the best formula for strengthening my desire to learn to swim. In fact, it only made me fearful. This fear, in turn, crushed my desire to learn. With my desire destroyed, I no longer worked to become a better swimmer. To this day, I have a fear of swimming in deep water.

Getting to my feet after my fall from the horse, I found myself in the same situation with Geoffrey—fearful.

Some months later, I visited my good friends Lynn and Steve Harris on their ranch in Cottonwood, Arizona. I talked with them about my being thrown off the horse that day in Cuyamaca and my growing fear of horses—as well as my increasing frustration with Geoffrey.

"Why'd the horse throw you off?" Steve asked.

"That's my question to you, Steve," I replied. "I was hoping you'd tell me."

"There had to be a reason," Steve responded. "Something wasn't right for him."

"Well, being thrown from the horse wasn't right for me!" I retorted. "My boyfriend was hoping that the more I rode, the more I would want to ride. The exact opposite is happening. The more I ride, the less I like it. And the less I like my boyfriend! Either I'm going to leave him, or I'm going to learn to love horses."

"Do you even like horses?" Steve, a bona fide "horse whisperer," asked skeptically.

"Not particularly," I moaned. "To me, a horse is just a big animal who poses grave danger for broken bones—mine. It's an unruly beast that needs constant feeding, watering and attention. Not to mention the amount of money required to keep the horse shod, fed, groomed, sheltered, and the vet bills paid."

"Remember the first time you stayed here at the house with us?" Lynn asked. "Our cat, Ippit, wandered into your room as you were unpacking. You glared at the cat and she instantly dashed from the room. Intuitively the cat *knew* she had treaded upon hostile territory. Do you remember that?"

"Sure do," I laughed. "I didn't particularly like cats,

then. I grew up on a large farm where cats were independent creatures whose jobs centered on keeping the rat population in check—you know, mouse patrol."

"What changed your mind?" Steve probed.

Thinking back, I answered, "My daughter probably had as much to do with changing my mind as anyone. When she went away to school, she begged me to care for her two kittens. But she knew she'd have to help me bridge the gap between my disdain for cats and my willingness to take good care of hers."

"How did she get you to do that?" Steve asked.

"She said, 'Mom, if you'll just take the time to get to know them, to learn a little about their basic nature, you'll fall in love with 'em,'" I recalled aloud. At the thought of my dear daughter's wisdom, I smiled with maternal pride.

"That's right," Lynn interjected. "Jennifer—a better teacher than your boyfriend, I might add—didn't just drop the cats off at your house and say, 'Live with them; they'll grow on you.' She took the time to teach you, to help you gain an understanding of cats. Do you remember specifically what she asked you to do?"

"Yes, it was actually a simple request," I answered. "Basically, she asked me to do two things: First, to observe them—I believe her words were 'watch how they *operate*.' Second, she asked me to notice how my *emotional presence* affected theirs. I remember asking 'What?' and she said, 'Mom, when you're in a good mood or a difficult mood, either way, it influences how I interact with you.'"

"Did you find her approach helpful?" Steve questioned.

"Very much so," I responded, now wanting to talk about the two little kittens who had become an integral part of my everyday life. "Even though I'd been around cats all my life, I had no idea they were such loyal, playful and affectionate little creatures."

Steve didn't want to hear about my kittens as much as he wanted me to understand what he was getting at. Continuing his questioning he asked, "And your emotional presence? What did you learn about that?"

"I discovered on those days when I was distant with the kittens, they shied away from me. On those days when I was openly affectionate with them, they would lie on my desk or, if they happened to venture outside, they brought their prey—a bird or garden lizard—'home to Mom.'"

"That's right," said Steve, slapping his knee as if he'd finally gotten through to me. "Jennifer was a good teacher. And, the more you learned about the cats' instincts, habits and interdependence with you, the more you started to genuinely respect and enjoy them. And soon you even looked forward to being with them, and enjoyed their antics at work and at play."

"Things were sure different with you and our cat when you stayed with us this past winter," Lynn interjected. "Do you remember?"

Of course, I remembered: It had been a remarkable difference. During that visit with Steve and Lynn, once again Ippit wandered into the room while I was unpacking. The cat and I exchanged glances. This time, instead of bolting from the room, the cat jumped up on the bed, nestled in beside my things and began purring. Instinctively the cat knew I wasn't an alien, nor alien to her.

"It's too bad that Geoffrey wasn't a more empathic teacher," Steve said. "I tell you what. I'm working with a couple, Todd and Sarah, near the Peacock Hill Ranch in Shadow Hills, California, next month. They're in a situation that's much the same as yours and Geoffrey's. I'd like you to come along and watch me work. I believe that if I can help you learn to understand and appreciate the basic nature of a horse a little more, you just might be inspired to try riding again."

"Okay," I said, accepting his invitation.

Little did I know just how much I would learn from the experience.

Sarah and her husband Todd had just married. While Sarah had grown up with horses and ridden all her life, Todd hadn't. She was hoping her husband would learn to share her love of horses but, after a year of riding, he was no more in love with "horse sport," as he called it, than when he began. I sat at the side of the round pen as Steve examined Todd's horse, a beautiful chestnut-colored Arabian.

"Todd, what do you see as the biggest problem or barrier to your becoming a better rider?" Steve asked.

"You're looking at him!" Todd responded, pointing at the Arabian. "This darned horse is stubborn and strong-willed. He's hard to catch. And when I'm riding him, he's more likely to do what *he* wants than what *I* want. Plus, he's overly aggressive with the other horses. It's a long list."

"The horse always knows what *you* know," Steve said, "and respects you accordingly. Let's just see what this

beautiful creature thinks about us, beginning with me."
Steve opened the gate and went into the pen. True to the
Arabian's character of intelligence, bravery, fierceness and
endurance, the horse arrogantly galloped around the pen,
occasionally kicking his heels into the air in an effort to
intimidate Steve.

"You can see by his actions that he wants to show me
that he's boss," Steve called to us. "Since I need to be the
boss, the first thing I have to do is to get his attention. I
need to get him to show me respect—in this case, it means
that I'm going to be the boss, not him." Within fifteen minutes of applying a technique he's developed in teaching
horses, one he calls the "touch of love," Steve was able to
give the horse simple commands that were systematically
obeyed. The horse lowered its head to knee level and his
tail rounded out (a sign of submission). With ears perked,
the horse now followed Steve around the pen, obediently
responding to his every cue.

Todd was amazed at the horse's changed behavior. As
was I.

"Okay, Todd," Steve summoned. "I'd like you to come
into the pen with me." Todd opened the gate and stepped
in. Upon seeing Todd, the horse once again galloped arrogantly around the pen, kicking his heels into the air, trying—and succeeding—to intimidate the man. Frightened,
Todd recoiled and quickly scuttled to the gate.

"Don't do that, Todd," Steve directed gently. "Come to
the center. The horse doesn't respect you. He knows he's in
charge and that you aren't. Almost everything we do with
the horse involves using a specific cue to ask the horse to

do something. If you don't have the horse's attention, you can't direct it. A wild mustang is generally easier to train than a domestic horse with years of bad habits precisely because it is attentive to your every move." Steve began teaching Todd. "To begin, stand at the balance point of the horse, which is just behind the center of the side of the horse. . . ."

I'm sure the session was insightful for Todd. It was for me. I learned things I didn't know, including what I had done wrong in the Cuyamaca Mountains that day when my horse reared to throw me.

My horse reared because it had been frightened. His instincts told him to quickly move out of the way of something, and he needed to look in order to make an assessment of what it was and what he needed to do next. And he needed his head in order to do this. In order for a horse to see clearly in front of it, the horse must arch its neck and draw in its muzzle in a collected position. In this instance, the horse needed more rein, not less, because the horse's vision is monocular (single-eyed), that is, the horse mostly sees its surroundings as two pictures, one from each eye. In order for the horse to have clear vision, peace of mind and security, it needs reasonable freedom to move its head and neck as it wishes. If the rider restricts the horse's head by holding the reins too tight—as I had done—the horse not only fights for its head, but, worse, panics. A horse will shy away sideways from something that startles it because it cannot tell what it is. The horse's preference is to turn and face the object head on, then from a safe distance look at it with both eyes and satisfy its curiosity. By pulling on the reins and forcing his head into the air, I restricted him from doing what he needed most.

My horse was saddled with two problems: the unknown object on the ground and the object in the saddle—me. Unfortunately, my horse couldn't resolve the problem of the unknown object on the ground until he got rid of the problem in the saddle. So he reared to dump me off. If I had learned this before getting into the saddle, I would have understood what to do. Rather than tightening up on the reins, I would have given him the slack in the reins he needed to see what was going on around his feet.

Later that month, I once again ventured down a Cuyamaca trail astride a horse. But this time my clearer understanding of horses rode along with me. When a pheasant squawked, jerked skyward and startled my horse—and my horse reared—instead of yanking on his reins I gave him more rein so he could see what had frightened him. My horse looked from side to side and assured himself it was the bird, not he, that should be afraid. He then huffed a sigh of relief through his nostrils. Settling down, he clopped on down the trail, his momentary panic alleviated rather than aggravated.

Lynn and Steve were pleased when—several months later—I told them about my newfound ability to manage my horse and myself in the saddle.

"It's an entirely new experience!" I declared, as pleased with myself as they were with me.

"And what *is* that new experience?" Steve asked.

"Well for one thing, knowing *how* to communicate my intentions and not impede or override my horse's ability to do his job has boosted my confidence," I explained. "And now that I have the ability to get my horse to do *what* I want him to do *when* I want him to do it, I'm really having fun riding!"

Steve and Lynn chuckled at my surprise—apparently they'd had no doubts.

"Thanks, Steve," I said. "And you, too, Lynn. You've helped me understand horses better and given me a desire to want to become a better rider." They smiled and nodded modestly, accepting my thanks.

"Hmm," said Lynn. "What about that boyfriend?"

"No," I said, "he didn't pass the test. I decided the way he taught me was largely about *his* nature, and that in life it's good to be with those who are compassionate and empathic teachers—those who grant freedom from fear, deepen *desire* and, thus, ability to learn."

20 Bashing Tony Robbins

"I'd like to be a professional speaker," Steve, the vice-president of a small bank branch, explained to me at dinner one evening. "Over the past few months, I've been looking very closely at the personal and professional lives of those in the industry. After careful consideration, I've decided I'd like to design a career that allows me the same versatility they have."

"Do you intend to give up your position at the bank?" I asked him.

"No," he said, "that's why I'd like to tailor a speaking career after yours. You spend as much time in your office as you do on the road. I want that balance. Besides, it'll help me keep my ego in check."

"What's that supposed to mean?" I asked.

"Well, I know what big egos professional speakers can get!" he replied, smiling coyly. "Take Tony Robbins, for example. I saw him at the sports arena last month. What an ego he has!"

I was surprised by Steve's comment. By his own admission he wanted to join the ranks of professional speakers, yet he was making disparaging remarks about one of the best professionals in the field. I found his imputations not only uninformed but unkind. "Perhaps you've misinterpreted his energetic style as ego rather than confidence in what he espouses," I suggested in Tony's defense.

"No, I don't think so," Steve countered. "I've never seen anyone pound his chest in accolades like that!"

I tried again. "Do you think he's ineffectual?"

"Oh, no, no," came Steve's reply. "I think he's an intelligent, successful and charismatic man. But I also think he's too self-exalting." Before I could comment, Steve added, "He should tone it down a bit, you know, less of the personal 'rah, rah' stuff. I have a poster in my office by Hildegard Knefin that reads, 'Success and failure are both greatly overrated. But failure gives you a whole lot more to talk about.' Not that Tony is at a loss for words, but I think he should downplay the success stories and elaborate more on lessons of defeat."

Steve's perspective got me to thinking: Why is it that some among us are more willing—and comfortable—

listening to personal accounts of chaos, disappointment, failure, even sorrow, than to personal accounts of direction, elation and success? It reminded me of an experience Doris, my friend Joan's mother, had on the publication of her daughter's book, a book that received a number of awards.

Joan's mother lives in a very small town where practically everyone knows each other. When the townspeople meet up with each other, a common denominator in their discussions is news of how and what family members are doing, especially the exploits of children. While standing in the checkout line in a grocery store one afternoon—the same day the local newspaper had released a story on Joan's success—several people in line with Doris commented on how wonderful it was that her daughter's new book had received such good reviews. For this group, comments were of the "you must be so proud of your daughter" theme. The people making the gracious comments were genuine and sincere about wanting Doris to feel their praise.

Others wanted to share in the glory of "one of *their* town's youth." For this group, comments centered on the adage "It takes a village to raise a child." Since everyone in the town—from teachers to store clerks to clergy—was a part of the outcome, obviously all had done their jobs well. Comments flowed along the lines of "*Our* kids (mine, yours, ours) are really doing well!"

Strangely, not everyone offered goodwill. One woman who normally greeted and chatted with Doris, stood one person behind her in the grocery line, staring aimlessly down the grocery aisle and absentmindedly taking inventory of the items in her grocery cart so as to avoid greeting

Doris. Still another checked her watch each time Doris looked in her direction—intentionally avoiding eye contact with Doris.

It's heartening that Doris received positive feedback and acknowledgments of her daughter's successes—and disheartening that she received blatant rejection from others. All were long-standing acquaintances. Over the years, Doris had listened to them tell of the achievements of their children.

"Why are you campaigning against expressions of success?" I asked Steve. "Personally, I agree with Harriet G. Lerner's comment, 'Telling personal experience is not just a matter of being oneself, or even of finding oneself. It is also a matter of choosing oneself.' Why shouldn't we talk of our victories and joys openly? They are the by-products of successful living and loving. Most everyone wants to be happy and successful, and in good measure, I might add. If you're down and out, people may listen but they don't want to know how you got there. But if you're happy and successful, they want to know how you achieved it. I don't think Tony boasts as much as *reports* on success. And yes, he often uses personal experience as a metaphor, but he shares it so that you and I might have the courage to try, to set goals, and—should we fail—to pick ourselves up, dust ourselves off and try again. Sometimes we succeed, and sometimes we don't. The point is we can't fly until we climb out of the cocoon. The hype is about encouragement and motivation."

"Well, he has too much hype for me," Steve retorted, adding, "and he's too hyper."

"I see it differently," I replied. "When people accomplish things, they're naturally excited and exuberant, and they project their energy. It is not a time to be self-effacing, but to share the possibilities and allow the rest of us to understand that these feelings and talents are also available to us if we will just step to the plate and swing at the ball. Just as we shout cheers when our team wins, we need to shout cheers when we ourselves win—as well as when our fellow man wins. If you don't believe in this concept, Steve, you might even be missing the point of being a professional speaker."

"What do you mean?" he asked.

"If you fail to share your joy and exuberance—the *feel* of doing, excelling, achieving and *being*—with others, why should others seek these attributes? If you have a passion for the way you live your life and for the goals you deem worthy, the *exuberance* of wanting these things is appealing and inspires others to want to excel and achieve for themselves. Even worse, Steve, if you don't share your passion and exuberance with others, it hinders others from sharing their successes and joys with you."

Two years have passed since that conversation with Steve. Still a banking officer, he is now a relatively seasoned professional speaker as well. Steve has learned firsthand the effects of openly expressing joy, optimism and the "rah, rah's" of success. Last month we met up at a national conference in New York City where each of us was a speaker.

"Sharing Your Successes?" I asked in shock when I noted the title of his presentation.

"It's my favorite topic these days," Steve said laughing. He then explained, "You were so right about needing to share our victories. I've had lots of experiences that bear that out, but one in particular really made it clear. I attended an important company dinner. Everyone got to talking about what was going on in their lives. It was like moan city. Each of my colleagues seemed to be in the midst of a crisis, major stress, chaos or challenge. While I'd had my share of tough times over the years, I was in a 'good space.' I'd had a great year and, to boot, I'd just landed a big account and was on my way to closing another. Life looked bright. The gap between what they were feeling and what I was feeling was major. At the time, it posed a real dilemma for me: I didn't want to make my colleagues feel bad by comparison, and I certainly didn't want to sound boastful. Talking about all my positives would, in the face of all their woes, seem like one-upmanship. It was a disheartening experience."

"What did you do?" I asked.

"Well," Steve said, "there's really not much you can do. I kept quiet, silenced for fear of making my colleagues feel inadequate. It was a lonely experience. It really brought to light your remark about how the positives in life need to be expressed every bit as much as the downsides. The more I thought about your words, the more I realized how important it is to share joy, happiness and success. I think it encourages others. I mean, why do we have to be apologetic when we achieve something?"

"That's right," I said. "Why identify the fruits of our labor as products of good fortune or an accident? It's like asking a hard-driving athlete like Jackie Joyner-Kersee, one of the greatest athletes in the world, to tell us her achievements are a product of luck instead of hours of training. If our children become positive and productive adults, would we claim that they are products of luck or accidents instead of products of our dedication and role modeling?"

"Well," said Steve, summing it up, "like a good friend of mine says, 'We can choose the affirmative and constructive, opening ourselves to a generous, loving life. Or we can chose the negative, limiting our choices, our actions and our dreams.'"

"Sounds familiar," I said. "Tony Robbins, right?"

"Yes, my *friend*, Tony Robbins," Steve replied, smiling. "By the way, I brought you something. I have a poster just like it in my office with these words by Nelson Mandela. They show how right it is that we portray ourselves as resourceful, hopeful persons, capable of creating, doing, being and becoming."

The poster read: *Who are we not to look to the good, for the good? Our deepest fear is that we are powerful beyond measure. It is our light, not our darkness, that frightens us. We ask ourselves, who am I to be brilliant, glorious, talented, and fabulous? Actually, who are you not to be? You are a child of God. Your playing small doesn't serve the world. There's nothing enlightened about shrinking so that other people won't feel insecure around you. We were born to manifest the glory of God within us. It's not just in some of us, it's in everyone. And as we let our own light shine, we unconsciously give other people permission to do the same. As we are liberated from our own fear, our presence automatically liberates others.*

What a wonderful declaration of being and becoming Mandela makes. Witnessing such celebrations in the "Tony Robbins's" of the world, we, like Steve, learn to more fully relish our own victories and joy—and liberate others to do the same.

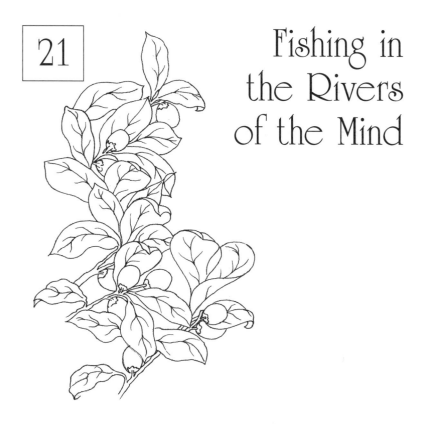

21

Fishing in the Rivers of the Mind

The room chorused with excuses: "I didn't do my homework because I didn't understand it." "I had to babysit my brothers and sisters, and my mother didn't come home 'til late." "I didn't have a dictionary at home." "I had a baseball game." "I was too tired." "I had to work." "I didn't have the money to buy notepaper." "My little brothers were making too much noise—I couldn't think." "My mother tossed it out with the garbage." "My dog chewed it up. . . ."

Taking note of their prolific aptitude for creating and relying on an infinite array of excuses—no matter how illegitimate they were—the principal, a tall, dark and soft-spoken man, began a yarn, one he'd told time and time again. "I once knew a boy who was one of fifteen children in his family," he said, eyeing each of the young people seated in front of him, "a family so poor that some days they ate only one meal a day. They lived in a small shanty, one so raggedy that the other kids pointed at it and made snide remarks when they passed by on their way to and from school."

The storyteller's name is Tom Lewis, founder and principal at The Fishing School, a Washington, D.C.-based school for youth. Seated in a circle of chairs around him, two students leaned forward, their chins propped in their hands, attentive to his every word. The other students slouched in their seats, intentionally unimpressed, expressions skeptical, if not belligerent. In an attempt to sweep the rest of the children into the drama of the story being told, the casually dressed giant before them bent toward the students, lowered his tone, narrowed his eyes and dispensed with his customary generous smile—as if to assure them that something important was to be learned there. "It was a tiny, old tattered house," he continued, "so small that the boy slept three in a bed—with his brother's big toe in his nose. But this was not the least of his worries. Not only did the other kids in the neighborhood talk about how poor this boy's family was, they also mimicked how the boy's father staggered while under the influence of alcohol."

"So his old man was a drunk," an unsympathetic teen jeered, causing an uproar of laughter in the classroom. Some chortled because this boy was a natural leader, and they knew he expected them to show allegiance to his every move and mood. Others laughed out of nervousness, the image—and ramifications—of an alcoholic parent too close to their own lives for comfort.

"Yes, that would be a fair assessment," the well-educated man replied earnestly. Looking into the eyes of the interrogating boy, he continued, "One time when he didn't have shoes to wear to school, his mother gave him *her* shoes. Well, you can imagine how the other kids laughed at him because it was obvious he was wearing a woman's penny loafers."

The room of hard-core kids thought this was absolutely hilarious, and hooted and howled at the boy's plight, exchanging rude comments—and anxious glances—about the boy and his mother. The man waited them out, studying the throng of faces before him—faces that reminded him of a time when he'd seen similar, though smaller, versions of these poorly parented children.

His memory offered up the scene in all its detail, one as fresh as the day it happened.

"Officer Friendly, will you be my daddy?" one small boy begged, grabbing the uniformed policeman's hand. "I don't have a daddy." Shoving aside another youngster, a third disheveled little boy wrestled for control of the man's other hand and shouted, "My daddy's in jail, and he's not ever gonna come home, so will you be my daddy?" Then, all squirming for recognition, the melee of raucous boys, two at each of his hands and three behind him, began to argue, "No! He's *my* daddy!" one insisted. "No! He's going to be *my* daddy, aren't you, Officer Friendly?" another disputed.

"No, he's *mine*," another shouted, pushing the little boy out of the way, and grabbing the man's freed hand. "Please, be my daddy. Please?" he pleaded.

The memory disturbed him—so much so, the storyteller had to willfully shake off his reverie.

The time of silence had been long enough for the much too streetwise adolescents to wonder just what he had up his sleeve. When the room returned to silence, the principal continued, "Even though this boy was from a poor family and didn't have much food or the right shoes and clothing, he was determined to make something of himself." Directing his words to the misguided young leader, the principal attested, "In all of life, no lessons proved to be more valuable to that boy than these simple lines he'd heard from his father. . . ." Pausing to give the children time to prepare for the importance of his words, the principal enunciated, "'It's up to *you* to turn on your dream machine and make a goal. It's up to *you* to be determined to reach it.'" Eyeing each and every adolescent in the room, he repeated, "It's up to *you*. It's up to *you*. It's up to *you*."

Looking into the bay of faces before him—adolescents who had accrued a long history of poor school attendance, course and grade failure, and worse, who held such low expectations for themselves that their futures would undoubtedly be dimmed, if not obliterated, by it—he paused and said, "Like many of you, the boy had it tough. Because there were so many in his family, he had to drop out of school to go to work to help put food on the table. And though he could have relied on a thousand excuses, he knew it wouldn't change his plight. It wouldn't put food on the table, nor hand him a high school diploma. It wouldn't earn him respect, nor gain him friends. He was sure he wanted a different, and better, life. Changing it had to start with a *conscious decision*; his life wasn't going to change on its own, nor was someone going to come along and change it for him. It was up to him. Like it is for you."

The young people, now deep in thought, sat quietly. Singling out each pair of young eyes, Tom said quietly, "The boy knew he had to take responsibility for all the choices he made. He had to start *thinking* about what he wanted out of life and setting goals. Though from humble beginnings, the boy did succeed. By holding three jobs, he eventually worked his way through college and found a good job." Glancing at his watch and surprised the time had passed so quickly, he concluded, "Time's up. I'll see you tomorrow. Do not be late. Do not bring an *attitude*. Do not bring any excuses for not completing anything I've asked you to do or think about."

As the kids filed from the room, they studied him with apparent deliberation. All remained silent.

Like the youths in the classroom, I'd listened to Tom's story with growing interest. "Tell me more about that boy from 'humble beginnings,'" I requested. Trading knowing smiles, I asked, "That was you, right?"

"Yes," he confirmed. "My parents knew that, given our situation, I'd have to make my own way. And though I did, their belief in me was an important part of the equation. I was lucky. Many of these kids don't have parents who are teaching them how to improve their lives, or how to be successful people. At least my parents instilled a sense of hope and encouraged me to 'turn on my dream machine,' set goals and strive to reach them."

As his parents had encouraged, Tom set goals and achieved them. After years of working odd jobs and putting himself through college, Tom joined the police force, where he was assigned to speak in the local schools as "Officer Friendly," a program designed to demonstrate to children that police officers were their friends, not their enemies. It was an experience that he never forgot.

"Morning after morning children would rush to shake my hand, pull on my pant leg, pelt me with questions— anything to get my attention," Tom said, shaking his head at the thought of them. "What I saw in those schools many wouldn't even believe. It was as if these poor kids had no one. They were just filthy, with ragged clothing, in need of a good meal—and a good bath. It broke my heart to see such helpless and seemingly hopeless children, all begging me to be their *daddy*. And I *knew* what the children in those classrooms where I spoke were going through: Many of my friends had no fathers. Though my family was poor, I always knew they loved me. Many kids today don't have this, and that's sad because these are essential ingredients. A loving family has been my greatest possession in life.

"Still, I *knew* what it was like to have other kids pointing and talking about me and my family and home. I *understood* what it was like to live in such bad conditions and to go to school and function in a classroom with other children who came from 'normal homes.' And, I knew that some of their parents—and teachers, too—didn't know the odds these kids were up against. It's hard to pull yourself up by the bootstraps when no one has taught you to tie your shoes, or worse, when you have no shoes."

"So a child needs 'shoes' before he can succeed?" I asked.

"Well, some programs try to remedy an impoverished background with handouts, but it's not the total answer. 'Something for nothing' can have a crippling effect because it traps people into expecting others to do for them what they must do for themselves. But they need motivation and know-how to go in the right direction. Food and shelter are basic necessities, but emotional support and human caring are also important. Just as painful as the filth and hunger I saw when I looked into the eyes of the elementary children were the looks of apathy, of feeling uncared for, of utter hopelessness. I felt a different solution was needed."

We exchanged murmurs of mutual recognition of these needs. "So you founded The Fishing School," I prompted.

"Well, not at first. My experience as Officer Friendly gave me a desire to be of service, to give back to the community in some way, to help others rise above their circumstances, but I didn't necessarily know what I wanted to do. I simply made a deal with God that if he'd let me have twenty years of successful service on the police force, I would retire and dedicate myself to helping others."

On Valentine's Day of 1986, Tom retired from the police force. Appropriate for the day, he dedicated himself to his own labor of love as he called it, dedicating his life to service. Retiring on a Friday, Tom kept that promise the following Monday when he began work counseling newly released prisoners at the largest halfway house in Washington, D.C.

"I was needed there, but even so, something was missing," Tom mused. "My heart and soul refused to be soothed by my work—purposeful and rewarding though it was. This bothered me, so one Sunday while in church, I asked God to help me sort out why I wasn't content in my work and if I should be doing something different instead. Instantly my head filled with the notion that I should show children how self-respect is earned. 'But how will I do that?' I asked God. As I lowered my eyes, I saw the words on the pamphlet in my hand, *If you give a man a fish, you'll feed him for a day; teach him how to fish, he'll feed himself for life.* I realized I was being called to work with young people—those whose lives paralleled mine when I was a child. And, I was to teach them to 'fish.'"

Hence, The Fishing School, where Tom is busy playing "daddy," baiting the poles of young people, teaching them how, in his own words, to fish in the rivers of the mind. In an atmosphere of hope, excellence and high expectations, Tom and his staff work with young people—all of whom are learning "to fish" for themselves.

Tom explained to me how that fishing is done. "We fish in the river of the mind for academic excellence with our after-school tutoring; fish for faith and hope with our inspirational program; fish for nutrition with our meals; fish for technical skills with our model rocketry and computer programs; fish for friendship and for general knowledge with our field trips and recreational programs.

"Our goal," he continued, "is to unlock the door and

break the cycle of poverty and deprivation. And to give youth a safe haven where they are free—if only for several hours each day—from the danger and despair prevalent in the urban streets. The program gives youth the tools to dream dreams, develop goals, and to fill themselves with hope and expectations for taking some control over their lives—and to not feel empty, useless or powerless to change what is, for some, pretty awful conditions."

While the full catch in the nets of Tom Lewis's labor of love can never be fully measured, a portion is witnessed in students who graduate high school, receive scholarships, and enter and graduate from college. As an example, recently one of his students auditioned and was accepted at the Washington School of Ballet where he performed *The Nutcracker*, a showcase that also provided him an opportunity to shake hands with the president and meet the first lady. Tom, his glow reminding me of a pleased father, enthused, "Since then, this young man has been accepted into the Dance Theater of Harlem." This young man, who sits in the second seat of the first row, is only fourteen years old! The boy across from him recently won an $8,000 college scholarship to a college of his choice!

"Some are harder to reach than others," Tom admitted. Smiling good-naturedly, he added, "I just keep baiting the hook and throwing out the fishing line. Few things can compare with the satisfaction of finally seeing those tough-to-catch ones brought in."

"Tom," I said, contemplating how much he had learned in his work over the years, "in all that you've seen, in all that you've experienced, in all that you've learned, what one pearl of wisdom would you offer? What advice would you give?"

Without hesitating, he replied fervently, "Parents need to stop making excuses why they're not parenting. It doesn't matter what the reason is: "His dad [or mom, stepparent, friends, others] counters the values I want him to learn.' 'I work and can't devote the time he needs.' 'He's unwilling to listen to me.' 'Television teaches unfit values.' 'I can't get him to turn the television off.' 'The schools have deterio-rated.' 'His teachers don't care.' 'He learns terrible things from the kids at school.' 'We live in a time of mixed mes-sages so what I teach is discounted.' Regardless, stop mak-ing excuses why you can't, don't and won't take good care of your children. No more excuses! Take full responsibility for your parenting." Meeting my eyes, he added, "Nothing would make me happier than to be out of a job!"

How fortunate we are that many children have been given a master fisherman—in their own words, a "daddy"—a taste berry to help them transform the excuses of real problems through the language of love, into goals and achievements.

But there's more going on at The Fishing School than meets the eye.

Quite often an early childhood experience becomes the playground for our adult years—one that brings the past into the present and can signal direction for our future. What we do, and most especially *how* we do it, often reveals not only who we are but what we *need*. When we heed the signals of our heart pointing us in the direction for fulfillment, we find our calling.

And so it was for Tom Lewis. Being a police officer inspired him to serve his community. Yet, there was an even greater mission than "service" brewing within, pressing for fulfillment. While Officer Friendly had been sent to the classrooms to effect change in the lives of the children, it was he who was changed. His words ring with sincere gratitude and wonder, reminding me of Richard Dreyfuss's line in the movie *Mr. Holland's Opus:* "Of all the changes I have helped bring about in others, the greatest change is what has happened within me."

The experience, by reawakening unsettling memories from his childhood, transformed his life, reeling him into his true calling. In the end, he found unexpected healing for *himself.* "There was something about my childhood that in adulthood kept tugging at my sleeve," Tom recalled. "It was as though the little boy, Tom, was not yet satisfied with the adult Tom. But not anymore! By playing daddy to children whose needs mirrored my own in childhood, I've appeased that little boy." Reflecting, he fondly remarked, "Every day, believe it or not, I am thankful for my childhood because it led me to what I do today."

A smile swam across his entire face, his eyes lit up with joy, his hands open, arms outstretched, as if embracing the world, Tom said, "Every day as I go fishing, I *know* I'm doing what I am meant to do. All of me is happy. All of me is fulfilled."

Tom, a fisherman of young souls, pats his heart, adding, "Even the little boy, Tom."

Such is the nature of *calling.*

22 | Something Extraordinary

"I'd like you to think about achievement," the seminar leader requested. "Between now and the next time we meet for part two of this seminar, identify someone who, in your estimation, has achieved something extraordinary. Keep your eyes and ears open—and biases in check. Successful people come in different sizes and shapes."

It was an interesting challenge; there are a great many models around. The first person who came to mind was Jackie Joyner-Kersee, two-time Olympic champion and world-record holder in the heptathlon, known as one of the greatest athletes of all time. Next, I thought of Stephen

Hawking, the Lucasian Professor of mathematics at Cambridge University (a post once held by Newton), whose brilliant mind has probed the frontiers of physics, astronomy and cosmology and given us a new understanding of the universe, black holes and quantum theory; Bill Gates, the information-age guru and one of the richest men in the world; Dr. Robert Schuller, Christian minister and spiritual leader whose ministry from the exquisite Crystal Cathedral and worldwide missionary travels have inspired spiritual seekers around the globe; and many, many others. So many came to mind that I decided to develop a list of traits to rank-order those I might consider and, in the end, select one from among them. In developing my list, I asked others what they considered traits and hallmarks of successful people.

"Respect, status and wealth are good indicators," said a colleague.

"The person's work or achievement is known in at least two countries," said another. "Living your life on your own terms," said another.

I especially liked the response of my secretary's fifteen-year-old daughter. "Oh, that's easy," she said. "Being rich and famous!" Having said that, she quickly amended it by adding, "And having a big house. And a boat!" Just when I thought she had completed her list, she added, "And lots of friends."

I listened closely and acknowledged the striving it took to reach the pinnacle of success in each of these achievements—and continued my search and exploration throughout the week. And then, just before I was to return to the second part of the seminar, I met Layne and Shauna, a couple whose success story is so grand—one that spelled "something extraordinary" so clearly—that they became my choice for topping the list.

Both Layne and Shauna are exceptional achievers, having chalked up a great number of individual accomplishments. Shauna Johnson is a three-time Olympic gold medalist in gymnastics. She is accomplished in tennis and skating and plays impromptu pieces on the piano, creating melodies of haunting beauty by ear. Layne is also an accomplished musician, favoring spiritual hymns and the organ. He has a twenty-four-year track record in his work (for J. C. Penney Company), and many trophies and plaques for his service and success in meeting goals.

Considering their vast accomplishments, I asked Shauna, "What do you think is your greatest single achievement?"

The couple looked to each other, smiled and then Shauna replied, "Our marriage."

"Yes," Layne agreed. "We're a real *team*. I think the best achievement is having a good relationship and a great marriage."

Though highly independent, Layne and Shauna pride themselves on the *unity* they share, the things they do in life *together*. They love cooking and frequently experiment with new recipes. Though each is accomplished in their shared passion for music, they value continuing education: both are actively working toward improving their skills. Twice a week they can be found walking hand in hand on the local college campus where they're both enrolled in classes. Ever so industrious, like many newly married couples their age, they dreamed of building their own home. This past year their goal was realized; Layne and Shauna moved into their dream home, a home they each helped to build!

His chest puffing up and smile stretching, Layne said, "We're being careful with our money because we're saving for a *new* car." With these words, he reached over and held Shauna's hand. Her eyes sparkled and her smile widened at his touch. The two exchanged a loving glance and he added, "Shauna's family is my family. My family is Shauna's family. And now we are our own family." When Pal, the dog member of the family, barked, perhaps agreeing, Shauna and Layne reached to pet him at the same time. Bumping their heads, they broke out in a moment of spontaneous laughter. It's obvious they are deeply in love.

"People have to think of each other," Shauna said softly.

"The most important thing is to help each other," Layne added. "You have to be kind and considerate. And never hurt anyone." Looking solemnly at his gold wedding band, he remarked, "Some people said we shouldn't get married. Sometimes people are wrong."

Layne and Shauna Johnson's achievements—individually and collectively—are all the more powerful and poignant when you consider that both have Down's syndrome. Down's syndrome is a condition caused by a genetic malfunction where an individual is born with one too many chromosomes. The condition causes individuals to share an uncanny resemblance to one another and a ceiling on intellectual potential. It also causes IQ to peak at around seventy-five, severely limiting capability and ability—or so doctors thought. When Layne was born, physicians recommended that his parents place him in an institution (the majority of which did little more than offer physical caretaking). The doctors' advice was, "Get on with your lives and forget that this child was ever born." Instead, his parents made the most of their lives, which included parenting Layne, expecting him to master the world in which he lived and helping him to achieve that mastery. Shauna's parents obviously did likewise.

Perhaps it is no coincidence, then, that when Shauna and Layne met, each instantly recognized how special the other was. Each also recognized the kinship each felt for the other. As a matter of course, they fell in love and married.

Two very special people, Layne and Shauna have both surged well beyond the commonly held assumptions regarding their potential and, by any measure, have achieved something truly extraordinary.

The seminar leader was right. To find and value extraordinary achievement we have to keep our eyes and ears open—and our biases in check.

23

Collective Potential

Dynamic, charismatic and energetic by nature, he was somewhat larger than life—more deity than man, though he was most certainly that, too. And though he wasn't quite at the top of his professional game, everyone predicted that he would be soon: He lived for the "next big deal." Bright, quick-witted and good-natured, too, and with no other standard than that of excellence, he was simply a force. Some women would have felt intimidated by him, some put off. Not her. She was drawn to these traits. She encouraged them. A striking blond, the epitome of an upscale, coastal California girl, she knew what she wanted in life and how to lay hold of it.

In keeping with their gallant personas, the dreams on their to-do list were as grand and intense as their passion for each other. Their goals were as bold and expansive as their zest and zeal for life. More than merely reaping the fruits of their efforts, they intended to devour the delicious morsels as well. They were going to live life fully—in their own words, "to realize *our* individual potential!"

Their game plan called for success in *every* arena.

One strategy in winning on a personal level included an annual renewing of their contract with each other—getting remarried. So each and every year, on the anniversary of their wedding day, they gather friends and family around them to celebrate another year of marriage together.

Each year, they invite me to join in the celebration. Each year, I attend.

This year was their tenth anniversary, and, from all outward signs, the vineyard of their goals had yielded an abundant harvest. The grapes of their efforts flowed forth, like a resplendent champagne. A toast was due. The occasion was planned to the hilt. Nothing was missing. In a room decorated with elaborate abandon, a popular band offered dancers a choice of jitterbug, waltz or salsa. The finest local gourmet chef sated guests' palates with a colorful and sumptuous buffet. Should a guest's choice of beverage include coffee, there was the leaded kind, decaffeinated or, if preferred, cappuccino, brewed in a large, gleaming, decorative copper tank. The twenty-plus desserts included twenty-five-pound bars of chocolate—both dark and white, with or without almonds—that were laid out with ribbon-streamered hammers so it could be chiseled off in pieces sized to our liking. From balloons and bouquets to the room full of "A-list" people from near and far, an enchanting stage was set.

I sat at a beautifully decorated table not more than five feet from the couple. As I looked at the comely "Barbie and Ken" duo framed before me by an elegant flower-draped trellis, I thought of the subtle changes I'd witnessed in each of them over the years. Still, I had no idea just how insightful this year would be.

The minister had known the couple for many years and began the program by sharing some of her knowledge of their personal experiences together. She then led them in their exchange of formal wedding vows for yet another year, concluding with the couple sharing with each other an informal "heart-to-heart."

He went first. Reaching into his sky-blue, exquisitely detailed and finely tailored designer jacket, he drew out a paper listing all of the things he wanted to say to her. Ever the professional speaker—and always theatrical—he first looked into the audience and smiled, then looked at his wife, cleared his throat, and with a solemn look on his face, scanned his notes of carefully chosen words. Hitching up his belt, he drew in a deep breath, squared his shoulders, looked once again at his wife, then at the pastor, and slowly, pretending to look for someone in particular, scanned the audience. As if to raise the suspense in the room even higher—if that was possible—he once again silently browsed over the poetic words he had prepared. Finally, as if now ready to deliver a major keynote address, he looked up and, with a beaming smile stretched from ear to ear, began reading the lovely words to her.

His wife, perhaps thankful that he had finally begun, rolled her eyes playfully, then relaxed her shoulders and released a big sigh. Now looking into his eyes, she smiled sweetly and listened intently to the melodic voice of the man she loved.

"I want my love for you to add joy to your joy," he began, looking at her and smiling. "To add peace to your peace. I want my love for you to beautify your beauty, magnify your magnificence. . . ." On and on he read, each phrase followed by another cliché commensurate with the others.

Perhaps she felt that the words were too composed, put together for the rhyme of it rather than the reason. Within moments, her lovely smile slowly faded and her eyes drifted ever so slowly from the mouth that spoke these syllables to his collar, to the bold multicolored tie, to the lovely canary yellow handkerchief in the breast pocket of his jacket. Slower still—so slowly that few noticed—her eyes, along with her now half smile, dropped to the floor.

I'm sure he must have picked up on it. Even so, all his customary aplomb and charisma stayed in place. He continued to read, but when he said the words "I want my love for you to glorify your glory," it was too much. She looked up at him and her face expressed a loving dismay. Ever so gently, she shook her head from side to side in a silent "No."

Like so many of us, he caught it, too. "No?" he said, chuckling ever so good-naturedly. His self-confidence was great enough to ease him through moments from which many would cringe. "You didn't like that one, huh? I did. I thought it was pretty good." He laughed jovially.

But he knew. He understood clearly that the pretty words he'd pieced together, though creative, didn't express the sincerity or breadth of the feelings they were meant to convey. In haste, he hurried through the remaining words.

It was her turn.

She reached into the archives of her heart and retrieved there an account of their lives together—a veritable ledger that thoroughly chronicled their common purpose and her deepening sense of appreciation and value for family, friends and community. Her summation of how lending a "helping hand" in his business had deepened her sense of connection to and her concern for the well-being of others the world over was eloquent and lucid. In simple heartfelt words she told him how profoundly thankful she was that these responsibilities were a part of her life, her work and her growth. Her promise of unquestionable love and support for him and all they stood for in their lives together was concise and precise. Her down-to-earth delivery of this impromptu and poignant presentation was so real, so earnest, so tender, so articulate that the audience was transformed from a state of merriment to one of heart-touched wonder. Many were moved to tears.

Her ardent words rendered his presentation silly, mawkish. He stood silent, looking at her tenderly.

I first met her nine years ago when he'd introduced me as his "dear friend and colleague" to his bride. About forty colleagues, along with our spouses, had been invited to a private and very special Christmas gala at the home of a mutual friend. With the exception of some of the newer spouses, we were all friends and peers and quite accomplished in our fields. Though his introduction of me was most flattering, she'd all but looked through me, considering me, I thought, unworthy of *her* recognition. At the time, I gave her the benefit of the doubt, deciding perhaps she hadn't yet developed confidence in being with such a professionally successful group of her husband's friends and colleagues. How she had changed!

Often it's the moments we witness outside the spotlight that are the most illuminating. This was certainly true the day of the renewal of their vows. Having traveled from out of town to attend this year's ceremony, I arrived early. So did the "bride." Wearing casual clothes, she made sure that all details for the event were in place. When guests began to arrive, she still had not had an opportunity to change clothes. Even so, rather than rushing to change, she personally greeted each and every one of her guests at the door, handing each guest a single rose and thanking each for being there. As the festivities began, she was right there playing hostess—hugging, laughing, greeting and seeing that all our needs were attended to. To assure that our every need and wish be attended to was *very* important to her.

Even at the ceremony, she was attentive to every detail in the room, including her two active children.

Perhaps for him this had become just another annual festive occasion and his last-minute, rushed creative prose was prepared more for audience value than the original intent: to honor this renewal of commitment. If that was the case, it would be the last time he took it so lightly. The wordsmith, the silver-tongued orator, a king of motivation had missed the mark. *Her* words—spoken with the power of love and delivered with passion—were much more profound.

And he knew it. In his heart of hearts, he knew that the words she had so easily spoken were those of great conviction. She had matured and grown more than he'd realized—a revelation that cut cleanly to the bone and to the real importance of their journey together.

He knew more.

She was just catching the spirit. There would be more to come from this sassy, witty, compassionate woman. He had only seen the *birth* of her calling. She was only beginning.

A man capable of great insight, he knew still more. For all the ways he had grown, he had miles yet to go. Recognizing her love for him and all the ways that it was manifested brought him face to face with an even greater awareness. For all his noble professional effect on the world, his greatest contribution was yet to come: to support and encourage her. And he wouldn't need to leave home or conduct a seminar or write a book to learn about it. The lesson was standing beside him. He need only love her. And if he did, she just might "glorify *his* glory, magnify *his* magnificence. "

Repressing the tears, he looked into her eyes and realized that the love and support she gave to him had been a taste berry of epic proportion. It sweetened his appreciation, love and admiration of her, their children, his work, and all those he came in contact with. Moving into her arms, he issued his most eloquent words of the day when he said simply, "Your love is a gift."

I know what a gift love is. But as I watched this couple hold each other, I understood more fully the extent of what love can do. In their commitment to each other, they had not only realized *individual* potential but *collective* potential as well.

24 | Cliffs Notes on "The Heart"

It was their tenth wedding anniversary celebration. Romantically, Paul and Polly talked, laughed and danced with an incessant closeness. "What a cute couple," the woman standing next to me in the buffet line whispered. "They look absolutely made for each other. They even *look* alike."

It was true: They did look alike. He just slightly taller than she, both with natural blond hair, fair skin and sky-blue eyes. I smiled in agreement as the beautiful couple was joined on the dance floor by their four children. The oldest was a handsome, curly blond-haired nine-year-old boy with an especially reverent and polite demeanor. He was followed by his feisty, flaxen-haired seven-year-old sister. Next came the baby of the family, a tousled towheaded toddler, looking every bit like Dennis the Menace. Finally, the five-year-old appeared, a serene and happy little dark-haired girl with olive skin and brown eyes—a child so *distinctly* different from the rest of the family that it was impossible not to notice.

Silently, I watched the woman's reaction to this scene of the whole family gathered together. "Well, they must have adopted that one," she whispered wryly out of the corner of her mouth.

I smiled to myself. "Hmmm," I murmured noncommittally, knowing that there was absolutely more than met the eye here. As I watched the couple dance, I recalled the days in college together when they had met, and the idealistic goals and dreams they had for their relationship together. They called themselves partners. The rest of us called them soul mates. They were the kind of couple who personified *ideal* love—and ideal commitment.

Even so, they would face an emotionally charged and heart-wrenching crisis.

With all the passion and dreams with which young lovers begin a new life together, they, too, resolved to always be close and united in all things. As it is with most, when their first child was born it was a time of celebration and adjustments. From all outward appearances, they seemed to manage very well. The birth of their second child added yet more adjustments, and again they met the impending challenges. They seemed happy and close.

Even so, two years later Polly's affair with a man with whom she was working closely resulted in the birth of a baby—a little girl noticeably different in appearance from the couple's other children.

As one might expect, a transgression of this magnitude is difficult for any couple to overcome. Likewise, the future of this couple's marriage was at a crossroads. Would they, could they, remain together? Could they work through the issues that this breach of their vows, and their trust in each other, brought to the fore?

I had been a part of his support system when he was sorting it all out.

"What an ordeal that was!" he remarked when we talked. "It was rough, *really* rough, but you know, though I'd never ask to go through it again, it was a *lesson* more valuable than any I could ever have imagined."

"A lesson?" I asked, wondering how he'd boiled it down to a learning experience. "What *was* the lesson?"

Looking at me, he recited earnestly, "Take good notes." Then he grinned and asked, "Do you remember whose line that was?"

"Of course I do! Mr. Kappan—Literature 300!" I answered, fondly recalling our college days together.

"That's right! It was Kappan's class," he confirmed, slapping my arm playfully.

The memory came rushing back. "Wow, did you ever take so many notes in all your life?"

"Well, his philosophy was that if we took good notes in class, we wouldn't have to study for the test. But after seemingly hundreds of pages of notes, rereading them in preparation for the test took about as much time as reading the assigned book which, of course, we never did. Or at least *I* didn't."

"So instead, we'd head to the bookstore and buy Cliffs Notes!"

"Yup," he agreed. "So that we could bypass all the verbiage and get right to the point—to the *heart of the matter.* That's probably how that axiom came about."

Remembering how very difficult this period in his life was for him, I asked, "Cliffs Notes on the *heart?*"

Looking pensive, my friend nodded and answered, "I needed to sort through the mirage of emotions, all the subplots, and get to the core of the story—the bottom line—to find out what really mattered."

"That had to take some serious soul searching," I commented, really feeling for him.

"That's for sure," he said and then explained, "For me, there were so many different emotions to sort out. I kept hearing different voices—each one equipped with its own loudspeaker—debating with the other about what I should do. It was pure chaos. I couldn't sleep. I couldn't eat."

"Voices? Sounds fairly schizophrenic to me!" I teased.

"Maybe so," he laughed. "Who knows just exactly how crazy we get when dealing with a partner's infidelity!"

"The voices?" I prompted, taking note how Paul often referred to his wife as his partner.

"There was my head talking, my heart talking, and the other voice, let's just call it my 'macho' side, talking," he replied, now able to articulate it. His blue eyes didn't flinch as he met my eyes with calm assurance, admitting, "At first the voices were all garbled: While one wailed in pain and grief and wanted to be held by my wife—wanting reassurance that all would be well—another screamed in resentful accusation, wanting revenge. Each of the voices wanted me to deal with the situation differently.

"My macho voice—my ego—roared the loudest. It reeled with accusations: *How could she do this to me? To us?* It wanted me to leave her because she betrayed me and the kids. This voice kept saying things like, *She's made her bed, now let her sleep in it!* I was eaten up with indignation, thinking, *I'd never do anything like this to her!* And I was embarrassed. I wondered, *How many other people know about this? What shall I tell them if they ask? What are they thinking about me now?* And then there was the other guy. *What did he look like? What did she need from him that I didn't have?* This voice produced some pretty rough times, and I realized that if I let the macho voice have its way, it would wreak havoc, playing on all my insecurities to a point where my self-pity and bitter pride would have taken me away from everything I love and want—my family.

"My ego saw everything—from my wife's transgression to my own course of action in response to it—as a matter of black and white. The second voice knew that things weren't that clear-cut. Thoughts from the voice I call my head were more analytical and more rational. It directed me to be reflective and exercise caution before taking any action, to ask questions like, *Am I willing to lose my family? What is best for the kids? Can my relationship with my wife be repaired, and if so, what can we do now to fix it and move on?*"

"I feel for you," I commented sympathetically, imagining his turmoil in being inundated with such poignant questions while in the midst of emotional crisis. "How did you sort them out?"

"I took a long hard look at our marriage and inventoried all the pros and cons of staying together," Paul responded. "I looked at the fact that she's a wonderful mother to our children and, in spite of her affair, she's been a loving wife to me, too. And the marriage goes beyond the house and home we live in—although losing that would be tough, too. My parents love her, as do my brothers and sisters. Plus, we've built a life in the community together. Did I want to throw all this away? We'd struggled together to accomplish goals that were important to the *both* of us.

"And I thought of the possibility of being *alone*. If I left the marriage, then what? Sunsets alone? Or do I find someone else, and start all over again? I'd have *this* home and *that* home, kids *there*, and, if I remarried, maybe kids *here*. I have men friends who have started all over again. Behind closed doors they'll admit it really isn't the solution." Growing reflective, Paul speculated, "Maybe that's what's wrong today. People just leave, breaking up a family, but that turns out to be tougher than fixing what went wrong."

"Paul, it's admirable that you were able to honestly look at what price your actions would cost, most especially to others," I commented. "How selfless."

Paul thought about my comment and then said, "I had to consider how my actions would ripple to others in the family—regardless of my feelings. I'm happy that I did. Caring about the needs of my kids and parents amplified the loudspeaker from the voice of my heart."

"The third voice?" I inquired. "Yes," Paul verified. "The voice in my heart was a very compassionate one reminding me that we're all human and sometimes frail. It advised me not to feel 'holier than thou' because she had breached our vows and I hadn't. What I liked best about this voice was that it didn't make me run around in circles. It zeroed in on the fact that I loved my wife and my children and didn't want to live apart from them. And it reminded me that what I truly wanted was the closeness and unity my wife and I once had. Cutting through all the emotional upheavals was helpful because, first of all, it didn't take up the energy that being scattered and crazy did, so I could focus my energy on working toward specific goals.

"The real breakthrough came when the reasoned voice of my head joined with the passionate voice of my heart. Combined, this voice asked me to evaluate my *leadership* role in my family—one in which I always prided myself in doing a good job. Needless to say, I had to reconsider my contributions to each family member. This time, the focus had to extend beyond paying the bills to making their lives better in other ways, beginning with my commitment to my wife.

"This voice also asked me to question what I believed about *love*. Did my love for my wife mean I love her only *as long as* she meets my criteria? Did it mean that I love her *if* she behaves the way I expect her to behave? Did I love her *when* she loves me the way I want her to love me? This led to 'Is it entirely her fault? Is there something missing in our relationship that made us susceptible to this?' If I'm honest, I have to admit that for more than a year before the affair I'd grown detached."

"But you were so close," I said, remembering what soul mates they were.

"It's easier than you think to misalign your priorities," Paul responded. "For me, that included everything from spending too much time at work to not taking a more active role in my children's day-to-day care." His eyes pinned mine and he continued, "Again, I'm not making excuses for her—or for me, for that matter. Taking responsibility for my part in this equation was difficult, and at the same time therapeutic. It was the beginning of my forgiving her, and also my asking her to forgive me for neglecting our relationship—all of which contributed to the walls and the distance that grew between us."

"Forgiveness is no small feat," I remarked. "And when we can't forgive ourselves we stray from the path of being able to forgive others."

"That's for sure," he concurred heartily. "I desperately wanted to forgive my wife. I just didn't know if I could. I didn't know what to do to lessen the feelings I had of bitterness, and hurt, and the deep sorrow I felt for the loss of the innocence of our love. Yet, I knew I needed to forgive. For one thing, I needed the personal freedom, the peace of mind. And I really did want to be at peace with her, too. Even so, though I knew what I ought to do, I didn't know *how*. I felt so deeply wronged and offended. It set up a deep internal conflict between what I knew was best and what I felt. But my heart kept prodding, 'You love her and you know she loves you. You *can* both get through this.

Your family is worth the effort.' And I'd yell back, 'How?' And my heart would repeat this impassioned plea, *Forgive her!*"

"*Talking* Cliffs Notes!" I teased.

"It sure seemed that way!" Paul replied, now laughing. "So, then I was faced with a choice: Was I willing to work with my feelings, honoring them while *directing* them? Or, did I want to continue wallowing in the pain and the misery of my bitterness, being directed by my erratic emotions? For me, it was a crisis of the will. I had to be able to deal with *me*, to manage me. If I wanted to move beyond this and reclaim my family, I had work to do—the process of getting what I wanted started with a conscious decision. I needed to focus on me."

Forgiveness was the silver lining to the cloud of being hurt. In *choosing* to forgive, Paul triumphed over the agony of feeling betrayed. The result was a deeper level of compassion and understanding of how to love.

"I respect and admire the depth of both your introspection and apparent application of a resolution to your crisis, Paul," I said. "You really worked at this."

"Yes," he responded resolutely. "It was largely the voice of my heart that allowed me to let go and forgive. And steered me toward where I am today—back together with my wife, both of us honestly working toward being happy and secure together. It's a whole renewed sense of commitment."

"Still," I prodded, "forgiving is not the same as forgetting. How did you forget?"

"I choose not to call to mind the hurt," he replied succinctly.

"Is that *really* possible?" I asked, wondering if he had reduced forgetting to "distraction."

"I choose not to dwell on the past or to obsess about what's been done," he answered. "The more you rehearse a memory, the harder it is to let go of it. I choose to focus on my children, *all* of them." Looking at the photo sitting on his desk of his children, Paul pointed at the beautiful little child bubbling with smiles, sitting amid her siblings. "Every day I see this beautiful child and every day I experience her love so every day there is a renewal of the decision to forgive. It gets easier and easier with time."

"And the other guy?" I asked, knowing I was treading in delicate territory.

"Oh," Paul answered kindly, "whenever I find myself caught in a web of jealousy or revenge or spiteful feelings, I remind myself of my choice to put it away. It's a sincere effort. I didn't just 'stuff it' as the psychologists say, nor am I in denial. I've simply changed the way I view it." Paul grew thoughtful and then added, "For all of us, our lives have a story to tell. In my life, the affair happened. It's a part of my story but it doesn't have to be the theme. I've reduced it to a subplot."

"So," I said, "the Cliffs Notes to the story of your life read, 'And then a little girl came along. . . .'"

Finishing the sentence without prompting, Paul added, "Renewing Paul and Polly's commitment to their marriage, to revamping their short- and long-term goals, and to co-parenting—lovingly while united under one roof—*four* very happy and spirited children."

"The end?" I asked.

His eyes softened as they once again found the photograph of his four children. He surveyed each of them, then focused on the face of the dark-haired one among them. "No," he said gently. "A little girl by the name of Joy came along—a little girl who is a complete joy—and taught his heart how to take good notes, in love and in life." His entire face smiling, Paul added, "And because of it, they all live happily ever after."

He paused and then asked, "See this smile? I can literally *feel* it. I love her very much. She is *my* daughter and a symbol of our family's strength."

The next day, I watched as he gently lifted the small five-year-old out of the passenger side of the family van. While in midair, she wrapped her little arms around him, buried her head in his neck, then grinned up at him and crushed an enthusiastic kiss on his cheek. He chuckled, hugged her tighter and set her on the ground.

The contrast was striking: He was such a muscular man, and she was such a delicate little girl. He was so fair, blond and blue-eyed; she was so honey-skinned, dark-haired and brown-eyed. These surface differences aside, their love for each other was readily apparent. Hand in hand, father and daughter walked to the back of the van, where she held up two little arms, wanting to help him carry the groceries to the house. He opened the van's door and carefully placed a five-pound bag of oranges in her waiting arms.

"Oooh, Daddy!" the little girl squealed, her eyes widening, her small oval face animated. "These are so heeaavy!"

He tossed his head back, erupting in delighted laughter. "Yes, they are, honey, but you are big and strong and can carry them," he said, bolstering her self-confidence by adding. "Can't you!"

Her giggles bursting to be turned loose, she replied emphatically, "I *can*, Daddy!"

Reassuring her sense of ability, he remarked, "I know you can!" Together they walked toward the house—with no break in either the small child's chatter or the man's rapt attention, their mutual adoration apparent in each of their faces.

Watching this touching scene between father and daughter, I felt the warm reassurance of his happiness.

Love—a taste berry of unparalleled power with an ability to transform all experiences—had made healing possible.

25 | Heroes Among Us

The sun shone brightly in the cloudless blue Wabash, Indiana, sky. "August 6, 1996 was an especially beautiful sunny day," recalls Jimmy Mitchell, a statuesque man in his early thirties. "I'd promised my two young sons, home on school vacation, that I'd have lunch with them."

He never got there.

Jimmy was following a man on a motorcycle who was behind a truck hauling a boat, when suddenly the truck swerved erratically. Miraculously the motorcyclist avoided hitting the truck, but he couldn't prevent himself from colliding with the boat.

The impact of the crash dislodged the boat from the truck and slammed the motorcyclist to the ground. In spite of the fact that the motorcyclist lay in the middle of the road severely injured, the driver of the truck never stopped his vehicle. Instead, he raced away from the scene of the accident.

Jimmy Mitchell didn't think twice about stopping to help. Nor could he ever imagine what price he would pay for his good deed.

"When I saw the motorcycle hit the boat and go down, I knew the motorcycle driver was in trouble," Jimmy recalled, his large gray eyes misting over as he detailed the events of his brush with death. "I pulled over, got out of the car and rushed over to give the man whatever first aid I could."

The man's name was Fred Griffin. After getting Fred untangled from the boat, Jimmy carefully dragged him into the shade, then told him that he was going for help, assuring him he would be back. Heart pounding with fear for the injured motorcyclist, Jimmy raced to the nearest house and asked the person who lived there, Charlie Neal, to call 911 and report that there had been a hit-and-run, and give a description of the truck.

"As it turned out, Charlie Neal knew Fred Griffin," Jimmy recalled. "Charlie made the call and then followed me back to where Fred was lying on the side of the road. Fred had broken his arm and ribs, and the gash in his forehead was bleeding profusely."

Jimmy was applying pressure to slow Fred's bleeding when, glancing up, he noticed that the driver of the truck had returned to the scene and was now tearing the license plates off the boat. When the man spotted Jimmy, he ran back to his truck. What Jimmy had no way of knowing was that the inebriated driver—a man with a criminal record—had returned to his truck to get a nine-millimeter pistol.

As Jimmy was bending over caring for the injured Fred Griffin, the man shot Jimmy four times, twice in the back. Thinking Jimmy was dead, the man then shot and killed Fred Griffin and Charlie Neal.

Within moments, another driver happened upon the scene. Billy Swan, who the night before had proposed marriage to his girlfriend, was en route to Indianapolis where he had a full-ride scholarship to a university there. Billy stopped to help. When Jimmy spotted Billy, he tried to alert him of the danger that lay ahead. "I tried to warn him, but my lung had collapsed and I couldn't speak," Jimmy said, his eyes wide and glazed with the same frustrated torment as his tone as he recounted those moments. "I tried to lift my arms to motion him to stay away, but my arms were paralyzed so I couldn't. Then I heard four more shots."

Believing that all were dead, the driver of the truck climbed back into his truck and sped away. He didn't get far. A roadblock had been set up in response to the 911 call.

Spinning the truck around, the driver raced back down the road in the direction of the accident. He tried to avoid the wreck he had caused, but in his frenzied flight, he rolled his truck and smashed into a telephone pole directly in front of Jimmy Mitchell. As he looked in the direction of where Jimmy lay, he realized that Jimmy was still alive.

"He was going for his gun," Jimmy said. "Thank God that in that moment a policeman arrived, jumped out of his squad car, and handcuffed and arrested the driver of the truck."

The cop's timing was fortuitous for Jimmy Mitchell. Even so, the gunshot wounds left the young husband and father of two small children permanently paralyzed from the waist down.

Jimmy Mitchell's tale was just one of the heart-wrenching stories I listened to while serving as guest expert on the *Geraldo Rivera* show. The stories of all the panel members assembled beside me—mothers, fathers and relatives who had lost loved ones to senseless violence—stirred my soul. Heroically, these individual family members rose above their despair. Like the Phoenix rising from the ashes, they worked tirelessly for the safety of others by initiating local, state and national reform, even though it was too late for their own loved ones to benefit.

Jimmy's story, like the others, was harrowing. But unlike the other panel members, Jimmy was an actual victim who had survived his ordeal. "You were so heroic, Jimmy. But after making such a personal sacrifice, would you ever be a Good Samaritan again?" Geraldo asked.

"I would help again," Jimmy answered without hesitation. "I'd want someone to help me. I think it's a sad world when we can't stop and help another person."

Of course, many people do stop to help others in need. Some are even decorated for their heroic acts, like thirty-four-year-old George Motza Jr. While fishing on a lake in Oxford, Ohio, George spotted a four-year-old boy who had fallen into a spillway and was in trouble. Leaping into the spillway, George fought the currents, swam to the boy and carried him on his back toward the bank. Another bystander grabbed the boy from George's back and pulled the boy onto the bank. Tragically, Mr. Motza was swept away to his own death.

This past year, George Motza Jr.'s parents accepted a Carnegie Hero Award on their son's behalf.

George Motza Jr. was one of many heroes among us who received an award and its recognition for their bravery and heroic efforts. Many do not. Like Charlie Neal and Billy Swan. And the citizens of Wabash, Indiana.

The story of Jimmy Mitchell, a man whose selfless act proved heroic, grows even more touching with the response of the citizens of Wabash to his disability. It was months after that fateful summer afternoon before Jimmy Mitchell was able to return to work. Many challenges confronted him. Confined to a wheelchair, mobility was one of them. After seeing Jimmy's wife, Lori, struggling to get Jimmy out of the car one day, Bonnie Corn and Idris Krynn, two other Good Samaritans, rallied the support of citizens in Wabash County to reach out. Members of the community opened their hearts, as well as their billfolds. Recently, on national television, representatives of his community presented Jimmy with the keys to a new van— totally equipped to accommodate his disabilities.

What is lost in so many lives and must be recovered is the trust that people will reach out to help, support and assist others.

Many do: parents who lovingly act in responsible ways in the raising of their children; teachers who maintain excellence in teaching their students to learn; friends who are caretakers and caregivers; those who act with honesty, courage, kindness, encouragement and plain old-fashioned courtesy—helping each other as we go about our lives.

Like Jimmy Mitchell did.

About the Author

Bettie B. Youngs, Ph.D., Ed.D., is an internationally renowned author and lecturer. She is a former Teacher of the Year, university professor and executive director of Professional Development, Inc. She is one of the nation's most respected and admired authors, with sixteen books published in twenty-nine languages and a number of audiocassette programs for Sybervision and Nightingale/Conant as well as the award-winning video-based training program for schools and parents, *Parents on Board*. Bettie is a frequent guest on television and radio talk shows including *NBC Nightly News*, *CNN*, *Oprah* and *Geraldo*. Her work has been recognized in *USA Today*, the *Washington Post*, *U.S. News & World Report*, *Redbook*, *McCall's*, *Working Woman*, *Family Circle*, *Parents' Magazine*, *Better Homes & Gardens*, *Woman's Day* and other publications.

To contact her, write to the following address:

Bettie B. Youngs & Associates
P.O. Box 2588
Del Mar, CA USA 92014

More Great Books From Bettie Youngs, Ph.D.

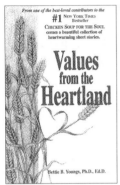

Values from the Heartland

Readers will discover the deeper side of integrity, commitment, honor, self-discipline, connection and character in this beautiful collection of poignant stories. It inspires us to remember that what is enriching and lasting in life is often the result of long-term investments in the people we love and care about.
Code 3359, $11.95
Code 3340, hardcover, $22.00

Gifts of the Heart

Youngs inspires readers with 27 real-life parables. These actual life lessons are genuine, potent and precious and show the process of the heart at work. All show the path to greater tolerance, acceptance, patience, grace, kindness and forgiveness.
Code 4193, $12.95
Code 4509, hardcover, $24.00

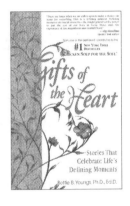

Safeguarding Your Teenager from the Dragons of Life

Keep teenagers on track toward worthwhile goals by providing the support they need to become responsible, happy adults.
Code 2646, $11.95